William Czappa

Trials, Tribulations and Triumphs of Running a Small Business

Why I sold my business after 35 years-
A Businessman's Journey To Liberation

The Agony and the ecstasy
(But ah… not so much on the ecstasy)

First Edition
July 22, 2018

Published in the United States by

ARC Publishing.
2800 N. Frederic
Burbank, Ca. 91504
(818) 846-5820 email czappasstudio@gmail.com
Web: czappa.com
or Google: czappa

Copyright 2018
William Czappa
All Rights Reserved

No part of this book can be reproduced without the permission of the copyright owner. The short stories included and others not included, are available for purchase for your promotions.

Photo credit; William Czappa
Cover layout; Patt Nicol

ISBN-13:
978-1725814844
ISBN-10:
1725814846

Copy writing pending, service request # 1-6804113761

Names have been changed to protect the innocent if any are similar it is purely by accident. Spelling errors may be intentional or just errors.

Copy 8-16-18 1:02 PM

Dedication

I would like to dedicate this book to all the wonderful customers that stayed with us through the years, recommended us and made it all possible. Also to all the employees that worked here over the years, some 125 of them. Many staying for the long haul, like Raul Ortiz, perhaps the employee of the century.

Also, Lloyd Zeigler, who lasted 17 years. I learned so much from all them good and bad and even gave me all the data for my book "Tech Techniques." I couldn't have written it without them. And I have to mention my landlord who didn't gouge me on rent, Dave Higgins and his mom, Clair Johnson, who passed away all too soon. Also, I have to thank LRH, who's technology made us last longer than most of our competitors. And lastly, thanks to my granddaughter Alyssa Magoon, Harry van Bommel and Nancy Branigan who did some of the editing on this book.

ARC TV 2012

About the Author

Czappa owned ARC TV electronics business in Burbank California for 35 years. William began his career repairing color TV sets in 1969 for RCA service company. After working there for several years he opened his first independent repair store, Frodies Place in Culver City Ca, where he grew up. In 1983 he took over H&G TV and ran that business for 35 years. He opened that business so that he could finance his art and writing career and not have to be a slave to the art gallery system.

William is also a California Visual artist and writer who has been making sculptures from found objects since the sixties. He began writing short stories in 1989 and began sending them to his growing art collector mailing list and then to his TV customers.

In 1987, The Burbank Leader first published one of Czappa's stories and for a short time he wrote a column for them writing short stories. Since then, over 25 of his short stories and other publications have been published in the Burbank Leader, the Burbank Times, the Tolucan and the Latest Magazine and on line.

His 50 year retrospective of his art work was held at the Creative Art Center in Burbank and February, 2016.
There are three documentary shorts on Vimeo and YouTube about William, his work and the shop. (*Videos of the retrospective and the documentary shorts are on the net. Just type Czappa Vimeo or Czappa YouTube*).

ARC also became ARC Gallery showing over 65 pieces of Williams work exclusively. The TV shop and gallery has been in several TV shows, like Storage Wars, and the Hulu show, Casual.

ARC Gallery 2012

Other books by this author are available on Amazon.com

Tech Techniques
A book about his 50 years in the repair industry. Rules that you learn the hard way.

Holidaze
A book of his humor short stories about vacations and Holidaze while growing up in Culver City Ca. and being a single parent.

Assembled in America
A book about is career as and artist with autobiography and 50 photos of his work with explanations.

Table of contents

1. The Beginning — 1
2. The Early Years — 4
3. The Good Years! Advertising — 6
4. What Happened? NAFTA Happened — 16
5. Update the Advertising — 20
6. The Learning Curve — 25
7. The Business Climate Changes, Greed sets in — 28
8. Employees — 35
9. Antagonistic Type Employees — 42
10. The New Generation — 47
11. The New Old Generation — 52
12. Great Employees — 57
13. Customers — 61
14. The Beginning of an New Era — 66
15. What Could Have Been — 69

Appendix

i. Why Fix Things — 72
ii. Pink Card — 75
iii. Flyer for New Customers "More Junk Mail" — 76
iv. 30 Day Thank You Letter — 79
v. Baseball — 82
vi. A full newsletter, "RCA Hollywood Christmas" — 84
vii. An anytime story, "Finding Ginger" — 97
viii. A summer story, "The Barbeque" — 102
ix. A winter story "Catalina Christmas" — 107
x. The Treatment for "Willies World" — 115
xi. The Economic Formula — 120

Chapter 1

The Beginning

It began July 1st 1983. I had been working for a small TV repair shop that had opened in 1969. It was called H&G TV, named after the owner Hy Gale, who used to say, "Little guy big wind." It's a mystery why Hy would be in that business, given that he didn't know how to even insert a vacuum tube in a TV set. And yes, there were still many TV sets back then that used vacuum tubes. But Hy relied on various technicians to come in and actually do the work. And by the time I showed up he was ready to close up shop. But with my skills and some fresh ideas the business expanded.

In those days, there were TV repair shops on nearly every corner. The phone book had 6 pages of ads because vacuum tubes had the habit of wearing out, so it was not uncommon to get to know your TV repair man. You might see him once or twice a year. Some adventurous people would take all the tubes out and go to Thrifty Drug Store, where they had a tube checker.

So, there I was working for him and building up his business. Under my guidance he started to make money again. And in fact the economy in the country generally was pretty good. You could actually make a great living repairing things. TV sets were very expensive so you didn't just throw them away if they broke.

After a few years of building up the business we were making so much money that we were investing in gold and silver bars. Part of the reason for that was, inflation was rising and you needed some way to hold on to your wealth.

Now the one thing that Hy figured out, was to put a small 5"x 7" pink flyer on everyone's porch. Every morning, before work, he would walk down different street and leave these flyers. The other reason he would do this was for the free fruit. Hy had lived through the great depression and as Groucho Marxs once said, "No matter how rich you are, if you have lived through a major depression, you will get up in the middle of the night, walk down stairs and turn off a light that you left burning."

So Hy would sometimes walk down the same street that had fruit tree on it and help himself to some fruit, even though they weren't even ripe yet. When going to a restaurant he would grab some napkins and also some crackers, stuffing them in his pockets. He wouldn't even throw away carbon papers from the receipts.

One tech that worked for him earlier on said that one day, while doing a house call, Hy saw some candy in a dish the customer had left out. Hy asked if he could have some and to everyone's astonishment emptied the whole bowel in his pocket.

He was always testing used vacuum tubes, hoping there might be a little life still in them. I discovered this one-day when I returned to work, having the day before repaired a TV that was now not working again.

What I found was a used tube in place of the new tube that I had installed the day before. But Hy was not able to even insert a tube in correctly and it was put in wrong with the pins all bent over. Sometimes people would stop by to buy batteries from him. He would excuse himself, walk next door to Smart and Final, buy the batteries, then walk back and sell them to our customer, marking them up.

Now I could see that the flyers were working but doing a house call for only $7.00 was a bit much. And this cheap price was drawing the wrong sort of customer. Customers that had some old crappy set sitting in the corner of their garage. I got him to raise the rate up and we began to make more money and get a better quality customers with sets that were actually worth repairing.

But, this was not a great work environment and since he wanted to retire, and I had just joined a group that had some great business technology that I was anxious to try out from WISE International, I bought him out. I cleaned out his desk, that was full of crackers and carbon paper, made the shop more appealing and being an artist, hung some of my work on the walls.

Now I have always been an artist and my first TV shop in Culver City was also my first art studio. So I thought naively enough, that I would expand the shop and eventually show up once a week to sign some paychecks and spend the rest of time in my studio making art. But that was not to be. Although when starting out as an artist one must have a day job, picking a complicated business to finance the art was going to turn out to be a very bad idea.

Chapter 2

The Early Years

Some things were easy back then, there were plenty of technicians to choose from, for one thing, parts were readily available. In fact, two companies would deliver them to us twice a day. And the VCR had just come on the scene. The early VCRs were very expensive so people wanted to take care of their investment. They knew that the video heads needed to be cleaned and listening to my customers concerns I printed on the other side of the flyer, we continued to pass out, a "Head cleaning special." It worked so well that for a while, every time I looked up another person was walking in with his VCR holding one of our special cards. We were on to something really good.

Now the early VCRs had sometimes as many as 7 belts and three rubber idler wheels. And as they wore out we would need to change them all. The cost to do that averaged around $135.00 and we would commonly get 30 of them a week.

TV sets were still expensive, especially if it was a TV in a wood cabinet, which made it an expensive piece of furniture. And, at that time, manufactures cared about the quality of their product and ease of repair. Quasar advertised, "Works in a drawer." You just pulled the drawer out of the front of the set and you could just pop in a new circuit board.

Later Zenith came out with the System Three that had only three boards. We could fix any of those sets in just 15 minutes flat.

The boards not only would be repaired by Zenith but would also be re-manufactured and sometimes even updated if the original board had too many re-occurring problems. We landed some big accounts with the Burbank, Glendale and Long Beach Holiday Inns. 20 or so TV's a month from them alone and all of them Zenith TVs..

Having landing that account, a new employee had been working for a company that rented visual aids, mics and amps to the hotels. I sent him over to the Holliday Inn and being that they were not that pleased with the company they were using, we landed that account too. We soon had many restaurants and convention centers using our service, like the Castaways. We were on a roll. We had to buy more rental equipment.

Real Power   Czappa

Chapter 3

The Good Years! Advertising

So this was great! Quality products and easy to repair. Units that cost a lot of money that people would keep and invest in and keep going. Our yearly income continued to rise. I got my first computer and began to write humorous short stories. I began sending them out to our customers as a newsletter. Just to keep in touch, give something back, something I learned from a new technology that I came across. I also sent everyone a thank you letter with a list of all the other things that we were now repairing. It was amazing to find out that someone who had used us to repair a TV set didn't realize we also repaired VCRs as well.

I also discovered a great way to deliver the door-to-door special to get new customers. I could print them up, put them in an envelope and have them stuffed in the Penny Saver magazine. Thus being sure they would actually be delivered, as the door-to-door delivery services often didn't deliver all that they said they would. Also, I didn't want to have to get up early and do what the previous owner did every morning. And I didn't need the fruit.

Using this new technology, I would put something catchy on the envelope insuring that people would actually open it. The first one was simply "Junk Mail" followed by, " More Junk Mail." And the most adventurous one was, " More Junk Mail" no need to open discard as is."

On that one, I got at least one person calling and arguing with me that I had made him have to open it.

Now the reason I put the flyer in an envelope was this, what are you thinking about when you go through your mail? You're thinking "Junk mail," Junk mail, junk mail" as you look for any important envelopes. When you see one that says, "Junk Mail" it duplicates what you're thinking and it makes you laugh and you just have to pull that one out and open it up. Because who would do such a thing?

I also learned from this new business technology that it takes about 6 weeks for people decide to respond to a flyer or offer. So if you are going to put out a discount for a limited time, it had better be good for more than 6 weeks. What I did was this, I printed on the flyer, "Good forever or the end of time." We actually occasionally got those flyers back many years later as I put a hidden date code on the offer so I knew when it had been sent. One showed up 12 years later.

I realized that your TV may not break every year anymore as when they became solid state, they would last longer. So if you wanted to get that work, have no expiration date on your offer. I also made sure the offer was on a small card. I would never put out a flyer on a piece of day glow paper. I wanted it to be small enough for people to see and maybe put on their refrigerator. And it worked!

There are other rules about mail as well, just for the record. For instance it has been surveyed that people will open up a letter that is sealed, with a stamp on it and hand written more often than one that has a mailing label on it.

Also a pink flyer or card will be kept more often than any other color. The list below is in order of how many will be opened;

* A sealed envelope, hand written address and a stamp
* An envelope with a label, sealed and a stamp
* An envelope that is sealed, stuck on label and bulk rate stamp
* A unsealed envelope with no address.
* A smaller flyer on glossy paper
* A 8 ½" x 11" flyer on day glow paper

Now the one thing that kept me from being a writer was the type writer. When my first computer showed up, with spell check and the ability to cut and paste, my writing career began. I could have done what Woody Allen does to this day, I guess. He actually uses an old typewriter but actually cuts and pastes the actual paper to change the order.

I began writing funny short stories about holidays and vacations. (Times my new technology called, "Pleasure Moments)." And boy did that work. I began sending them out to our customer mailing list. I would do a holiday story before the holidays and a second one about summer vacations around June or July. I then put on the other side of that story a list of all the growing services that we now offered.

And later I turned it into a two page newsletter, where I could point out helpful tips, like, never wrap your potato in recycled paper because recycled paper has particles of tinfoil in it and it can make the heating element, (the magnetron) fail prematurely. The reason you wrap a potato in paper, then get it wet by the way is, it keeps the skin moist.

So now people were really paying attention and would never go somewhere else, because we kept reminding them we were here.

Some would tell me that they forgot who they used last and kept the newsletter so found us again. Many others reported making copies and sending them to friends and relatives. One customer said, when they went camping they would read my stories around the camp fire.
(You can see some examples of these newsletters and flyers in the appendix).

And how did I pay for all this advertising? I found Itext. It's a trade organization where you trade your service or product with other members who are also in the system. For a 10% cash charge to Itex, you could sell your wars and then use those credits to buy things you may need, like printing. I even got my first computer on Itex, rented a place to stay in Hawaii, got my vehicles repaired, dental work, acupuncture and even a case of wine one time.

I then found a printer and another company, that was also on Itex, that would stuff and seal the envelopes. And much later found an even better company We Mail for You that would print the envelopes and newsletter, stuff them, label them and even mail them out. Now all we had to do is send them the copy and the mailing list, via email, and that was that.

At the end we had 14,000 people on our mailing list.

As it got larger we would divide it up. And as customers returned for service, we would put them at the top of the list. Thus, if we later didn't want to do the whole list, we would be hitting the most active people. Although it's a good idea to mail to the oldest people on the list as well, sometimes, because you never know who might become active again. And they may not know you now offer new services or products. So if you are buying a business, the mailing list is one of the most valuable assets.

There are different types of advertising for different types of customers. A news letter is designed to keep the customers you already have and make sure they know what new service or sales items you are carrying. Many times people would forget who they used and I would get phone calls asking if we were the shop that put out the newsletter? They remembered the newsletter but forgot where we were located, or they never came to the shop, as we just did a house call for them.

The 30 day thank you letter, is to not only to let your customers know about everything else you do, but reminds them that they only have 90 days guarantee on any parts we installed and 30 days on the labor. You want them to tell you if something is wrong before the parts warranty runs out. Because, after that point, someone is going to eat it on the cost of the part.
And you don't want them to give you a bad review on the internet. The last thing you want is to have an unhappy customer that doesn't mention it to you.

So, that letter also encourages them to communicate with you so it can be handled.

The Junk Mail letter is designed to find new customers. It gives them a reason to fix things and a list of all the things we do. By the way, I realized that we could milk other cities like Tujunga and Sunland. They were cities that are an upper valley from us and there is no direct road to get to them. The only shop up there didn't have a great reputation and those people would drive into Burbank for service. As other shops went under, I also found out that people would come into Burbank from the Hollywood area too. So sometimes you get lucky and can tap into a neighborhood market with a Junk Mail type letter.

Now, on Yelp and Google, they just give you a web page and you should always claim these free pages and put up some photos of the shop or products you make and hours of operation etc. These sites are also great for getting new customers. And they usually pull in a good quality customer, because people trust other peoples recommendations, so those customers are often easier to deal with. That is, if you have a good reputation, which is the reason for the thank you letter, so you can handle any complaints before they give you a bad review.

Now the new owner advertised on yelp in the past with success. He said he now is spending about $300.00 per month. But he doesn't know really how much work actually arrives from that investment. It is important to know what advertising is working, so you don't waste money. One way is to just listen to your customers, they will sometimes mention how they found you. I would get at least one person a day mentioning our newsletter for instance.

Sometimes, especially before the phonebook ads would need to be renewed, I would put a survey list on every phone and try to get all my staff to ask every customer how they found us. I would make a list of all the various ways people could find us, phone book, our web site, recommendations and from whom? Yelp, Google, etc. That way the staff person could just check it off. It was hard to get them to always do that, even when I scotch taped the form to the phone handle so they wouldn't forget.

Not surprising, the newsletter always came in first, then recommendations from other shops and then, finding us on Yelp. I never paid for a Yelp add, but did put a free discount coupon there, so I could see if it was working. Of course you know that it's working because people will email you directly from that site. Those emails have increased over the years as more people use Yelp.

The new owner, though, found that we were getting calls as far away as Watts and we are located in Burbank. That would normally not be an advantage to drive that far for a service call due to traffic. Going to Simi Valley though, would not be as bad because there was never any traffic going that way, if you went early of course. So even though you can tell Yelp what area you want to advertise into, they may not put you in the right area and you'll be charged for those calls anyway. That probably happens more often if you are in a business with little competition. Because in order to get enough calls funneled into your business, they may have to extend the area. And it's to their advantage to get as many clicks as possible, since they get paid for each click. So, once again, the importance of doing a survey.

A Holiday card we sent to our management companies.

So with a great advertising plan in place, we were doing really well. So well that we needed more space. Our shop was only 600 square feet, and since big screen projection TV sets were coming on the scene, we needed more space so we moved up the street to a 1700-foot shop. We could now not only do big screen TVs but also microwave ovens. A local business, Thrifty Washer and Dryer, didn't like to do microwave ovens because they were more electronic and worked on 5000 volts (Older TV sets work on 32,000 volts). We were used to dealing with that. So they began sending us these customer's as well and also small appliances, which they didn't do either.

Now we had all kinds of room and a lot of space to put my ever-increasing art collection. Yes, It was the hay day of the electronic repair industry. It is not a great idea to have two unrelated businesses in one space. Generally it's frowned upon, but somehow it worked. People would stop in to see the art work, because I always put the newest piece in the large front window. Then ask what else we did and we'd picked up repair work or duplication work.

It also eventually pulled in three different videotographers who made documentary shorts about my work and the shop. The last one can be seen on Vimeo, just type *Vimeo and Czappa.*

It went to the Hollywood, Dances with Film, film festival where I saw myself on the silver screen and had to be interviewed afterwards with the other vidiotografers and people in the other films. That documentary also went to the Burbank Film Festival and the Savanna Film Festival.

It also later was pickup by the National Geographic's Short Film Showcase. It became a staff pick on Vimeo and was reposted around the world. If you type my last name and Vimeo 10 Google pages come up, at least at that time anyway. But not one sale related to this video. The other documentaries can be found on YouTube and the art work can be seen on my web site: Czappa.com or Google czappa or
https://fineartamerica.com/profiles/bill-czappa.html

The other interesting thing was one of our customers, who was a successful actor, loved my short stories. And he told me that if I worked up a treatment for a TV show, although he couldn't guarantee it would be picked up, it would at least be read by someone important. So I dashed off a treatment for a show based on a true story, me and the shop. It was about what I was going through each day trying to make it as an artist, yet having to deal with my staff and customers. Pretty much everything mentioned in this book. If you want to know what day to day life was like at ARC, just read the treatment. (*It's included in the appendix*).

I sent it to him and never heard from him again. Later we did some charity work for another executive from CBS. Apparently they loved my stories too, and when my newsletter arrived, they would be forwarded to all the different departments. I was told that when I had an art show, the art department would make up a large poster promoting my show and hang it up at the studio.

So he gladly agreed to read my treatment too. But there was no reply, maybe it was too racy, maybe the spelling wasn't good enough, maybe it was too ahead of its time, because I would put in a "Reality show type segment" in the middle of a typical sit com? *(You can read the full treatment in the Appendix and decide for yourself).*

But, Although we were doing well, over all, that was all going to change.

Promo piece by; Serena Creative

Chapter 4

What Happened, NAFTA Happened

NAFTA happened, that and many other trade agreements that would eventually destroy the repair industry, seemingly overnight. VCRs had dropped in price to $125.00 and not many years later to $50.00. We were now pitted against the cheapest labor forces in the world. They could manufacture a TV cheaper than we could repair them.

But let me tell you a story about two of my fraternity brothers, to give you an example of how this hurt other businesses.

Chuck and Jack were having lunch at a Charthouse Restaurant. And they were discussing ways of meeting woman, when Jack noticed the fresh cut flowers on the table. He asks the manager who provides these flowers?
He's told that the person who brings in the vegetables, also brings the flowers from downtown LA, at the Farmers Market. Now they only cost maybe fifty cents a table, but look how many tables there are and how many Charthouse Restaurants there are. Right then a business was formed. They paid a visit to the flower market downtown and realized they could buy the flowers cheap, hire some woman to cut and arrange them, then Chuck would once a week, deliver them to all the restaurants. And best, they could hire and would meet woman.

Jack then talks to the CEO of the Charthouse Restaurant chain and lands all the accounts. His stint in business school had paid off. Off they were, except they didn't do their home work. After stopping by the first Charthouse he discovered that in just three days the flowers were wilting (even though the restaurant each night would put them in the cooler).

So going back to the flower market, to do more research, they discover that they had bought the wrong flowers. They needed ones that were more durable but more costly. But, there was still quite a profit left and so they had to re-buy the flowers, pick them all up and redeliver the heartier product.

From there Jack then went to all the other restaurant chains, landed all those accounts and they were now rolling in the dough. That is until NAFTA. When people were losing their manufacturing jobs, the restaurant industry was also going to suffer. Because eating out is a luxury someone out of work doesn't have. All the chains switched to dried flowers and they found themselves and their staff out of business.

Rudy, another fraternity brother of mine, had started a business making the best vehicle alarm on the market. The failure rate was less than .1%. Whereas China's failure rate is around 10%. Cheap products took his business from 35 employees to him, his partner and one other employee. And then they were gone. As the economy dropped other businesses also held back and cut corners on things.

We had been servicing all the security time lapse VCRs for Disney. Some 60 machines that needed their heads cleaned three times a year and heads changed once a year. In an effort to cut costs, they replaced all the VCRs with computer recorders that didn't need heads or cleaning.

We had the NBC account and would go to the studio lot and pick up VCRs and TV sets for service at least once a week. One reason for losing that account was due to changes they made in their business structure and many departments were closed. So they would just take those VCRs and TVs, as they needed them, from the closed offices, instead of repairing the broken ones.

And the Holiday Inn instead of buying TV sets decided to lease them, so we lost that account. Good thing, because the next generation became harder to repair.

About this time an article appeared in the Wall Street Journal. A writer went across the USA to see how small repair businesses were doing.

He discovered that 50% of them had folded due to cheap products. Companies that repaired everything like printers, air conditioners, lawn mowers and cameras. He even brought in things for repair and discovered that his printer just needed the print head cleaned. A very economical repair.

We had overnight become a throwaway society. The only good thing, at this time, was the movement to stop all the dumping and filling up our dump sites with toxic and lead heavy electronics.

Peice De Resistanc   (The French spelling) Czappa

Chapter 5

Update the Advertising

When things go slow you always get moving on your advertising. I realized that our customer base was made up of people who didn't believe in just throwing something away when it broke. So, I added a short letter on the other side of our letter for new customers, "Why Fix Things." In effect it said,

Well, at a time when we are being asked to separate our garbage for recycling, why are manufacturers urging us to just throw away that old TV monitor or VCR -- not recycle it but dump it in the nearest landfill? Just throw it away, even though it's full of toxic material, including lead, and other chemicals? Are the manufacturers actually urging us to just dump it, even though special precautions are now made (at huge expense) to get lead paint off of a house and have it carefully dumped in special toxic control sites? Not to mention there is now an added mandatory toxic fee charged on new TVs and monitors.

Besides the toxic issues, just consider for a moment all of the wasted energy and resources that go into making any of these products. Metals, plastics, IC chips, PC boards -- all made using our resources and energy. Not to mention the Styrofoam, cardboard, and fuel necessary to ship it, usually from Mexico or China. All to deliver you a poorly made product that now lasts only one or two years, and all too often, only six months. Then, you, as a consumer, are given the privilege to drive down to your local discount store and start all over again.

Wasting more resources to acquire another product that may not last as long as the one you just tossed.

And consider this, another 30% of all broken VCRs, CD players, DVDs, fax machines and printers are not broken at all but just need <u>a good cleaning</u> and nothing more.

(The full version of this letter is in the appendix).

Now this was working pretty good, as I discovered that 1/3 of the people believed that you should get all you can out of a product. Another 1/3 thought everything new was better and improved. And 1/3 was being swayed by the other two groups.

The middle group thought this because computers were always getting better and faster, but they were not lasting longer either. Hard drives and all your data was going to be dumped at a much sooner rate. (Don't forget to back up your data on a regular basis). But other products were just being made flimsier.

They were being made so badly that there was even a warning, in one of the owner's manuals of one make of VCR, that said, you should not push the cassette in too hard or you could damage the machine. And, you had better put it in straight as well or that could damage the machine too.

I got the "Why Fix Things" letter printed in the local newspapers and on other places on the now growing internet. It wasn't long before everyone seemed to realize this.

People became disappointed that their brand new and expensive, LCD TV was only going to last 3 years before needing service.

They had become accustomed to a TV lasting 5 or even ten years before needing service. I can't tell you how many times someone would say they still had an older TV in the bedroom that was 15 years old and never needed repair. And of this writing, we see cheaper makes only lasting a year and don't expect better makes to last more than 2 or 3 years.

Millions of older picture tube type TV sets, that had years of life in them, sets that would last longer than the new set they just bought, were going to be dumped! You couldn't give them away.

Let me talk about toasters. We would get toasters in that were made in the 40's or 50's and just would need a new cord or a switch cleaned. But some of the new toasters were made with a small circuit board that tripped a relay. The circuit board would go bad in just a few years and that part was not made available. And, in fact around that time, there was an article in Consumer Reports that said, "If you buy a new toaster don't expect it to last more than 3 years!"

I saw a video on Facebook where there was a TV monitor in the door of the refrigerator, another in the counter top and another on the front of a cabinet. If they ever did try that you would need an extra room in your house for the repairman to stay in, because the way things are made today, you would always be repairing them.

And things just aren't being made better or smarter. The washing machine and dryer with a knob that you just turned, is the ideal switch to control either of these appliances. But what they've replaced it with is an electronic circuit. The last thing you want in a device that has heat, moisture and vibrations is an electronic circuit.

In order to make microwaves look cool, they made the control panel look like a cell phone touch pad. Looks great, but in just 3 or 4 years that part can cost $400.00 to replace. And that's just the cost of the part. Putting the keypad in the door looks great but that just makes it harder to repair and thus costs more to fix. The simpler way is almost always the best way.

And while talking about microwaves. Why didn't they standardize the mounting brackets or at least the mounting holes that go on top? On some machines, they put them so close to the front and sides, that in some homes, you could no longer mount them using those holes. Had the engineers also become stupid? Yes, they did. You know the best engineers are ones that have to go into the field and repair or install things, so they would know what us techs were running into.

For a time we were getting in TV sets where the circuit boards were coming unsoldered. When they make a two sided board, they have to connect the circuit on the top part of the board to the bottom part of the board. And what they use for that is something I installed on my very first job at Acutech in Marina Del Rey. I installed griplets. A small fitting that a gripletting machine snaps into the circuit board.

I didn't know it then, but many of those griplets, that I was installing, were going to come undone. The problem is that as the board heats and contracts, it tears the griplet apart even though it's soldered. You can re-solder it and that will last for awhile, but it will just come apart again. I discovered a cure for this. You would drill a hole next to the griplet and solder a wire from the top to the bottom of the griplet. So as the board expands and contracts the wire just flexes and doesn't come undone again. Some GE sets had 140 griplets that had to be repaired that way.

Interestingly enough, in our trade magazine appeared an article that GE had spent $100,000.00 to figure out how to fix this problem. They came up with a similar solution to what I had come up with. I could have saved them a lot of dough. And as other manufactures made the same mistake, we already had the cure.

One Single Dot   *Czappa*

Chapter 6

The Learning Curve

I also discovered that when a new product came on the scene, there was a learning curve. At first it's over built, way too many parts and thus it's expensive. These units are bought by more wealthy people. Then they come along and figure out how to make it simpler. And those units are at the peak of quality. They are dependable, easy to repair and quality units and the price comes down, but they still aren't cheap. But then, the third stage comes along. The last stage is, they're going to build them for "The Masses." Now they have to go back and make it cheap, cut the quality, get rid of unnecessary parts and bring the price down so the masses can afford them.

The similar thing happens to computer programs. They start out crude, get better, then they get perfected. But they want you to buy the next program so they have to screw it up and make it do more things that you'll never use and turn it into a piece of crap that's hard to use. I noticed ads on eBay for a Quicken program that said, "This is the older version, before they screwed it up."

So new is not always better. And that was one of the biggest problems about being in business was trying to keep up with the changing programs. You get a new program and everything is different. You now have to learn where everything is and how to use it all over again. Computers were supposed to make our lives simpler, remember that?

This led me to one of the tech rules in my tech book. "Don't think the engineer was logical" You get a new program, DVD, TV or remote control. You try to find how to label the inputs, for instance. The tech rule says; After you try to find the most logical place that item should be, go back and look at the illogical places that it could be. If that doesn't work open the owner's manual, but don't think that will be laid out logically either.

But when these products started to be built overseas and in Mexico, the quality began to suffer. Manufactures suddenly didn't care about quality any more. Zenith used to say, "The quality goes in before the name goes on." The first brand new Zenith TV we received from their new factory in Mexico, we found the Zenith label had fallen off. And the bottom board on the cabinet was a piece of pressed wood that looked like someone found lying in the street dirty and all banged up.

The manufactures didn't care anymore and it was no longer possible to call them for technical assistance. They wanted all the repair work for themselves. Zenith cancelled us from being a warranty service provider and bought their own service trucks. The whole business climate was different now.

Even though we had been a Zenith dealer from the start, we couldn't get the same price as the big box stores. I called Zenith on this once and asked why Circuit City was selling a TV for $50.00 less then my dealer price? I asked if I bought a 1000 of one model could I get that price?

No, I was told, they're a "national" buyer and I would have to open a shop in other states to qualify for that price. So the writing was on the wall. A small business was not going to be able to grow and would need a huge investment to get over that hump.

You see before this time there were laws against undercutting your competitors in order to drive them out of business. But that all changed due to corporate greed and the new Walmart philosophy.

And what geniuses at Zenith thought it would be a good idea to change the name to LG? I can only wonder how many sales we might have lost due to that stupid idea. Not to mention all the time we had to use up trying to explain it to everyone.

Chapter 7

The Business Climate Changes, Corporate Greed Sets In

The whole business climate was changing. A new business model was coming on the scene. Large corporations discovered they could buy the government, change laws to their advantage and wipe out smaller businesses. Sometimes they didn't even bother to buy government; they just made back room deals. Monopolies had returned.

Sony and Hitachi made a deal with Sears that if they sold their TV sets for only a $50.00 mark up, they would give them a bonus on top of the $50.00 bucks. This went on for years and wiped out some 27 American manufactures of TV sets. Zenith sued them over this and they got, as I recall, just a $100.00.00 fine. But it was too late for most of those manufactures that failed. Next thing we new, Zenith gave up too and moved their factory to Mexico.

If you don't know the story of Walmart let me enlighten you to what they did. Their business model was to put a huge mega store in a small town, whip out all the local shops, then close the mega store, because the town would die. The only people left would be the gas stations, the bar and post office to serve the farmers that couldn't leave.

Then they would build another mega store in another town and do the same things. All the people left, that couldn't afford to leave town or were farmers, would now have the privilege of driving 35 miles to the next Walmart to buy their goods. Empty towns all across America now sprang up. You see them all the time on that TV show American Pickers, empty towns. Amazon can do this without building a mega store but hurts businesses in large cities too.

When a mega store moves into a small town, it sucks the money out. Because large corporations are more efficient, higher less people and buy in large quantities, it's impossible to compete with them. So the small less efficient shops close. The ones that hired more staff, at a higher wages, go under. All the money in the town leaves to the corporate headquarters in some other city.

The other thing people don't know about Walmart is, it's a lie that <u>everything</u> is cheaper. One ex-executive spilled the beans one night on 60 minutes. He said that they would have a stack of really cheap $59.00 microwave sitting in the middle of the isle. People look at that and think, "Wow, they do have great prices." The problem is, Walmart knows that no one wants that piece of junk. They know what people want. So the one that people do want, is overpriced, because people don't bother to check. I checked and we often could match or beat a Walmart price on the items people wanted.

But we did have a huge advantage. Not only were we more knowledgeable about the products but our stock was shipped directly from the manufacture to our air conditioned warehouse in Van Nuys. Shipping TVs long distances in rail cars and un-air-conditioned warehouses, can lower the life of a TV. All that heat and vibration is not good for flat screen

TV sets, as parts of the display are connected to the board with tape. And if this tape comes undone you get sharp lines in the picture. Usually it comes undone after the warranty period, of course.

The other thing that I noticed was, beside NAFTA, even our city government was starting to work against us too. They first helped our competitor, Circuit City, build their store in Burbank by giving them a huge tax break. Then, some years later, they gave Costco the choicest piece of land right in the heart of our city and also a huge tax break, so they would move their store to Burbank. Why? Burbank would eventually get a cut of the sales tax they collected, that is, after their huge tax giveaway expired.

What did the city do for us small businesses? Nothing! Well, I can say they did one thing; they finally realized how these megastores affected the smaller businesses and fought tooth and nail to keep Walmart out. But, Walmart ran an end play and simply bought a Sears store that had failed, and then there they were. If small businesses are the backbone of the American economy, then why are they trying to kill small businesses?

For the first 10 years or so, our advertising budget was very little, now in the mid nineties, in order to keep our yearly income from dropping even further, we had to increase our advertising budget considerably, just to keep it from dropping too fast. But drop it did. Many companies go under because when things get bad they stop advertising. With the new technology that I had been studying, I knew that was the wrong thing to do. And so we saw our competitors dropping like flies. That did help but not enough.

And in the end, I could open up a phone book and there was now only ¼ a page of TV shops left, when in the beginning, there were 6 pages of TV repair shops listed. Under antenna and microwave ovens, we would be the only one. Good for us, as we didn't any longer have to pay for large expensive ads. But we had some advantages too and moved into other areas. We specialized in phonographs which made a comeback and our DVD and film duplication part of the business was doing well. But we would not turn anything away, now doing everything from toasters, hair dryers and even mechanical Christmas decorations.

And Yelp, Angie's list and Google came along. Free reviews by our customers, as long as you were doing good work anyway. And while on the topic, if you get a bad review answer it. Often I found that it was not justified. The unit was out of warranty or had a new problem that the unit was not brought in for. I would always have a look at the service record, if someone brought something back, and go beyond the warranty, when possible, or at least give a lesser charge if the problem was a new one. And it's important on Yelp, Angie's list and Google, to thank everyone that gave you a good review as well.

The major companies, now that we were in the teens, began to make some parts for LCD TV sets so expensive that it would, sometimes, not be economically practical to repair them. They also began to violate a law that said, in California at least, on any product over $100.00 parts and service data had to be made available for 7 years.

Enter eBay and the market for used circuit boards picked from sets with bad displays. And there were companies who repaired the more common boards and that kept the price down to. We also used eBay to sell off un-needed stock and began selling items for other people who were not computer savvy.

One year I sold 15 very expensive base guitars and a B7 organ for one customer. I think we grossed $25,000 on those items alone. I sold so much that year that eBay gave me a special phone number to call, just in case I had any problems.

We then entered the market of safely collecting broken electronics and having them safely disposed off. The government didn't want all the lead and other chemicals in electronics being dumped in our waste sites. So we made a little extra money collecting those broken units.

It also made it possible to not have an expensive dumpster. People also gave us some fine working units, because they wanted them to be used and not just dumped.

Another area that I had problems with, beware of automatic re-newels. Even though they have to make it easy to stop them, dumpster companies and phonebook advertising companies would stick in, that very long contract, an auto renewal slot. So if you didn't remember to cancel the ad you were stuck for it for one more year.

And the most irritating thing was, credit card processing companies. They all promise a low rate but in just a year or so it rises. Then the next one offers you a low rate and off you go again. I thought I found a good company because it had no bad Yelp complaints. But that was because they were new. Just a year later I checked again and they had complaints too.

And never lease the machine. Your rate may be lower for awhile, but you will end up paying $2000.00 for the machine by the time the lease is over. And then you have the option to buy it for even more money. You can buy them outright for $600.00.

One last irritating thing that happened was this, the radio stations turned corporate. You need some music when you're repairing things. Listening to TV is horrible, especially cartoons or soup operas. Instead of the variety of music, that I grew up with on the radio, they all started playing the same 50 songs over and over. I got so feed up with this one day that I called K-EARTH to complain. I actually got to talk to the music director. I asked her how many times do I have to listen to Sugar Shack and Louie Louie, just two of the songs that were being played over and over at that time.

She told me that lots of people like those songs and they pick songs by survey. They play 10 seconds of various songs and people pick which ones they like. I said, "That's the problem! Doing a survey like that, you're only going to get songs that people already know. There are lots of songs that are great, but you would have to listen to them longer to appreciate them because they're not being over played!" She says, 'Oh, we know that people only listen in for an hour." I said, "Yes that's why! They can't take listening to the same songs over and over again. That's why they don't listen longer, they can't take it anymore"

There are great songs that no one knows about, like Simon and Garfunkel's "Papa Hobo." *"Got a hell of a basketball team, got a left handed way, of making a man, sign up on that automotive dream."*
I asked so many employees if they have ever heard that song and not one of them had. One didn't believe that there was such a song, I had to bring in the sheet music to prove it to him.

Interesting, when I visit a friend in Clearwater Florida, there were still stations that played a mixture and variety of music. When I visit him there, I have to turn the radio off before I go to bed, because they're playing so many great songs, you don't hear anymore, that it keeps me up.

And of course this happened because so many of the independent stations were bought up by corporations and what do they know about radio? Corporations seem to ruin everything they touch. We had a stationary store that had everything, all kinds of templates, stick on letters everything I needed, killed, by the big box stores. I went to Staples and Office Depoe to find vinyl stick on letters for my outdoor sign. Neither one stocked 6" numbers. They had letters, but no numbers. Didn't they think anyone would ever want to put a phone number on a sign? I thought, did they both hire the same guy to buy their stock for them?

Chapter 8

Employees

In the beginning it was easy to find people to work for me especially techs. But there were also new techs that came from tech schools like ITT Technical Institute. The problem with these schools was, they gave theory but no hands on experience. The first tech I hired told me that in his class the students wanted to bring in a TV and at least open it up and see what was inside. But their teacher would not even allow that.

I was getting people who thought they had training, but in fact, had very little useful knowledge. I would hand them a circuit diagram and they couldn't tell me where a voltage originated from. Or, I would hand them a voltmeter and they couldn't figure out how to use it. But since they had their degree, they expected a huge wage. I was going to have to teach them everything.

The problem is these schools didn't have any practical training, so immediately, once they tried to fix something, they were in trouble. It would be like training a secretary but never teaching her how to put a piece of paper in a fax machine.

So we ended up with a lot of characters. There was Ron, a smaller thin guy, who spent most of the time holding his cup under the coffee maker, as he couldn't wait for the coffee actually make it into the pot. But Ron had lots of car trouble.

At one place that was repairing his car, they had a fire while his car was there. Another time he had gone to my mechanics home to drop off his vehicle in Chatsworth. I get a call from him, he's stuck at my mechanics house because my mechanic was so tired, he laid down and Ron couldn't wake him up to get a ride home. He had to spend the night.

And there was the guy who lost the keys to the service truck the second week of work. Not to mention the guy who only lasted 1 hour. We sent him to the bank to do two simple things and he only did one of them.

There were also two shocking incidents. But first I have to say, it became illegal to do a lot of deep checking of new employees. You could only check their driving record. That told me a lot sometimes, DUIs lots of parking tickets etc. But that was about all.

The other employee, in fact my first employee, had some run-ins with the law previously but seemed to have straightened his life out. And after leaving my employment, started his own business, got married and even had a kid. But it was not to be. He thought it was a good idea to go to Van Nuys, pick up prostitutes, have sex with them, then spank them, but not pay them either. I think it was the not paying them part that put him back in jail, this time for life, because of the three strikes law.

And so things like this could happen too. There I was sitting watching TV after work, when two police officers and two detectives come knocking at my door after work.

After talking to them for a short while, the detectives let the police officers go, as they realized I was not the person they were looking for. After describing my employees to them, the newest one fit the bill. We went to my shop and looked over our delivery schedule and realized he was in Van Nuys the day the crime was committed. He had stopped somewhere, forced a woman into the delivery van and had sex with her. Now, to show how dumb criminals can be, the delivery van was painted like the war bonnet paint scheme of a Santa Fe Diesel engine. So it stuck out like a sore thumb. They also had other evidence from the inside of the truck, like some tools and my brief case.

They wanted to interview him and I had gotten him to do some courses at the organization that was helping my business, so they went there to interview him. I had to let him go for that and the fact that he couldn't remember things I was trying to teach him. He did do some time in jail and some years later called me saying he had now become an insurance salesman. The police impounded my van, tore out my brand new carpet for evidence and I had to pay towing and storage fees at the impound yard.

So there were a lot of things that I learned about checking people out. One was, never hire someone who has a bumper sticker on his car that says, "Don't get mad, Get even."

The person who taught me that lesson pretended to trip on some wires in the shop. But instead of reporting it, (didn't even tell his wife what he was up to), instead went to find an ambulance chasing attorney, which he found. Now he had been out on a friend's boat in the Marina and thought, "I'd like to have a boat too." So the scheme was hatched.

He found out that if you filed a claim with workman's comp insurance, they would settle with you for $12,000.00 to make you go away. Because if you went to court and won, they could be milked for life, that is his life.

But I still had to go to court to testify. He walked in not even bothering to limp. The workman's comp attorney said that was typical, he would limp when he got in to see the judge. He got his $12,000, minus attorney's fees but didn't get his boat as planned, because he owed child support to his ex-wife. She got the boat.

Another rule was not to hire someone who just came in from another state. Because soon as the holidays rolled around, our busy season, they would get home sick and want to go home for the holidays. By the same token, if someone has to drive a long distance to get to work, given the traffic in Los Angeles, that was going to be a problem.

And people using bicycles for transportation. Now if they are doing it for exercise, that's one thing, but if they are doing it because they can't own a car, because they can't afford it or because of driving issues, that's another. One bicycle riding person was going to work for me for just a couple hours a day.

I hadn't really hired him yet and thought, that wouldn't be enough time to get much done, so I didn't hire him. He asked to use the bathroom and left a little turd on the bathroom floor.

Later it became illegal to even ask certain questions when you put out an ad. There are all kinds of things you can't ask. Some of them I agree with. So, because of that, you just have to take a chance.

One employee was walking really slow. I asked him one day what would happen if he walked faster and he said, "I might fall over." He didn't have a handicap that I new of.

Some people are just slow. Sometimes going too fast can also be a problem. I move quickly and there are some customers who just can't handle people moving too fast, it upsets them. So with these types, I would have to slow down, move slower, talk slower, then everything would be fine. One of my dogs is also like that, he doesn't like it if I walk too fast through the house.

Another person I hired early on, was also on welfare. He asked for $10.00 and hour but he was not a trained tech and as far as I could see was not worth that much. And at that time, around 1985, that was a lot for an un-trained person. I asked him why he needed that much and was told, "If I don't get paid that much I would lose money because welfare would cut my benefits." So now I was competing with the welfare office.

Just because the person worked for a major company may not mean much. I thought Burt might be a great tech because he had just gotten out of the air force and was working on their expensive jet airplanes. But after one week I could see that he would be a dangerous person to have around because he was losing tools, parts and service slips. I asked him what the air force did to make sure he didn't leave a screw driver inside the engine or in the electronic bay. He said excitedly, "Oh we had a board and every tool had to be put back on that board before the plane could take off." I said, "Great! But how would they know if you didn't make sure a plug or connector wasn't fully snapped in place ?"

He had no answer for that. It was about this time that jets where suddenly going out of control and crashing. Dean Martin's son was one of the victims and I new why. This guy wasn't qualified to repair a lawn mower.

Now West was one of the most interesting characters I ever met. He was an old time TV tech from the past. He apparently didn't feel high voltage. He would dazzle us by letting electricity from old TV sets hi voltage tube arc through his fingers. A one inch arc of electricity from the output tube of an old tube type TV set would surge through his body and he was oblivious to it.

Since your body measures some 100,000 ohms, he would simply lick his fingers and put them over a resistor that was of similar value and the radio or TV would come to life. He would use his body as a component. Much faster than using a voltmeter, but not a recommended technique.

But one day, my employees heard sirens out front and realized that West was the victim. He had legally crossed the street, got hit by a car and traveled through the air some 20 feet. I learned later, unbeknown to him, that the lady who hit him was not a hit and run and she had insurance.

I thought the hospital might want to know that bit of data, since they would be paid, but they didn't care. Even West didn't know that he was covered. No one from the city government told him. So I went on line, put the case on a web site that attorneys can access for new work and Voila, I found a great attorney for him.

He was even willing to pay West's car fare to his office over the hill in LA. He even advanced him some pocket money. He was going to make some $35,000.00, minus attorney's fees. So I took him to the Burbank police department, to get the police report, and he was off and running. After that I never saw our heard from him again. He still owes me a few bucks.

Chapter 9

Antagonistic Type Employees

Over the years I realized that there are different types of employees. And one type you get a lot of, are ones that cannot follow the most reasonable instructions. It isn't that they can't remember, much worse than that. They are intentionally not following orders. One indicator is, they have to do everything their way, which is usually the wrong way. It's as if they are working against you and have to overtly argue with everything or just quietly not do what you asked. And you had better understand that they <u>are</u> working against you.

Interestingly, they can also be the owner of a company to. They'll even destroy their own business. You see them sometimes on those TV shows like the *Profit* or *Kitchen Nightmares*, that try to help failing businesses. They argue with any reasonable new idea the host comes up with and usually, after the show ends, they go back to their old ways and often go out of business anyway.

If you detect this type of person it's a good idea to get rid of them as they're not there to help you at all. If you find you are working for one of these types I would quite. Any great new ideas you have will be squashed.

One such person was doing odd jobs for me and had just painted the dash board of my delivery van. He new about paint and primer and such. I thought he might be this type of person. Because of that, I gave him special instructions to paint just the outside of the sign on the shop. I stressed not to touch the main part of the sign where the letters were, just primer the outside because if it's messed with, (the part the letters were on), the whole thing would have to be redone and that part of the sign was fine. After coming back from a service call I noticed he had painted the wrong part of the sign and it would now have to be all re-painted.

Another one was a minister in his church. I get a call from one of my customers complaining that, while on a service call to fix one set, they had him take another portable set to his house to fix. But he didn't fix it right. I called and asked him about the ethics of doing that and he said, "Well they didn't like your price so I offered them a lower price if I did it." I could only guess what ethics he was teaching the people in his church. He just stopped coming to work one day, but had no problem filling for un-unemployment insurance anyway.

Now Clyde was an interesting character too. He had worked installing cable lines for the cable company. I would've thought he was good at it, being that he knew the numbers of the various ladders and even brought an orange cone to put behind the service truck, even when it was parked in our parking lot.

But then one day on a house call, he can't fix the set. When I get to the house, I find the cone neatly placed behind the truck, but entering the living room, he has all the service caddies laid out and parts everywhere. He was putting on a show for the customer. He couldn't fix the set because he had not noticed that he had installed the module upside down.

And even though he had been installing cable lines, on one antenna job, he ended up with a rats nest of wires all clumped together stuck to the side of our customer's home.

He also suggested that we finely detail every unit that came in. Instead of repairing things he was more interested in cleaning them. We did do some cleaning but detailing a TV takes time and is not workable.

But what we didn't know was he was also very prejudice. My bench tech, Allen, was from South America and in fact a very good tech on the bench.

The training schools there, unlike here, had actual on the job training. After they learned the theory they would actually go and fix things. But not only that, they would then have to train the new techs as they came up the line. So, with this system in place, that school was actually turning out great, fully trained techs.

Clyde didn't like this one bit. Allen would come in early and Clyde wanted to also come in early. But Allen didn't open the shop when he came in and he had no instructions from me to let other people in.

So Clyde asked if he could come in early too. But before I had a chance to tell Allen this, Clyde comes to the shop, the very next day, and bangs loudly on the front door, Allen comes to open it and Clyde gets him all upset saying, "Why don't you go back to your home country."

This sets Allen off and I get a phone call from Clyde saying, innocently, "I don't know what's wrong with your bench tech, he's spitting all over the floor."

When I arrive at the shop, I find out what happened and get Allen calmed down. But I can't get Clyde calmed down. He had expected me to fire my best bench tech right there on the spot. When I didn't Clyde just kept getting more upset and we had to send him home. After numerous calls from Clyde asking to come back, and saying he would just avoid Allen, I had to let him go.

Chapter 9

The New Generation

But cheap products were also drying up the supply of trained technicians. They were going into other fields and the computer was now king. So many of the people who would have gone into our field were now heading for the computer field. I think it was around 1995 that I was no longer able to find an outside TV technician. There were still jobs with the larger companies out there because they could offer benefits, but they were most likely operating their service departments at a loss.

In the first years of the new century something else started to happen. Since I couldn't find trained technicians, I thought maybe I could train people myself. So I sought out people who wanted to learn the business. Some of them had goals to be in other fields like computers, or the entertainment industry, so what I could teach them might be useful to their eventual preferred careers. Some had gone to recording school but couldn't even hook up a stereo? They were trained in a studio but apparently never taught how to hook things up. Who did they think was going to do that for them?

Dave, a friend had a business that cleaned business offices in those huge buildings with thousands of offices. Out of frustration with the same problem of trying to train people, he tried this.

A young man shows up for a job. He says, "Come on down here" getting on his knees. Dave picks up some dirt from the floor and says, "You see that? That's dirt." He looks around and finds some more, picks it up and says, "See that, that's dirt." He then says, "Now you find some." The young man looks around finds some dirt, and Dave says, "Good, find some more." He does and after doing this a few times says, "This place is filthy." Dave says loudly," Good, now clean it!"

The problem Dave realized is people just don't see. They just don't see what's in front of them. So they just don't notice things. So Dave said, "You just have to make them see."

But what I also kept finding is people who could not remember things. And some of these people had bachelor's degrees. I wondered how they ever made it through school? In researching this I discovered two possibilities, one was the use of marijuana, a side effect of this drug is memory loss.

The other cause, I suspected, was energy drinks. They also reportedly caused memory loss too. So this was something that I could not ignore.

And the new younger generation had different ideas about work. I recall a segment on 60 minutes that showed larger companies having to give this new generation special training. Like, when you get hired, you cannot take a 3 week vacation two months later. Or, you cannot come to work late, go out back and have a smoke, then spend an hour checking your personal emails. One tech I hired to train in May, told me after a month, "Oh by the way, I'm going to be spending the summer in Japan." It's very costly to train people. It takes time and they can be counted upon to make costly mistakes that the shop has to pay for. It's a major investment and you hope to get a return on that investment by them staying for at least a year or two.

I was talking to a fireman one day discussing this issue. He said that they would send one of these younger people to bring them a Phillips screw driver and they had no idea what that was. They were also shocked to learn that they would have to polish the fire truck!

So the government forcing us smaller companies to train people, at an ever increasing rate of pay, was going to be a major problem. The tech schools were doing a lousy job of it and ripping off their students with huge student loans.

I started getting people who owed 30 to 60 thousand dollars for student loans and I couldn't see anything valuable that they had learned.

They had been ripped off royally and now somehow us small businesses were supposed to find the money to invest in their training? I'm all for raising the minimum wage, but there should have been an exception for small businesses or some sort of training fee re-imbursement if you took on someone to train. It became so bad that, bill collectors were calling me trying to get them to pay their student loans.

One guy never gave me his full name and address because he was afraid his pay would be garnished if he did. Years later I kept getting credit companies calling for him trying to check references, as I guess he was trying to get more loans.

So now, because these people with memory loss, could not remember polices, I was now getting all the problems those policies were there to prevent from happening all over again. It did give me a new rule for my Tech Techniques book though. Companies write policies up to prevent a problem from happening again. "If you leave the barn door open the chickens will get out." So don't leave the barn door open! If you are a new employee or manager or you just bought an existing business, to be successful, you must read or find the existing policies and apply them. Because if you don't, you get the problem all over again that the policy was there to prevent from happening in the first place.

So, now with their memory loss, I found myself running around putting out fires all day.

At one point I even had to sit two employees down and make them practice their handwriting because I couldn't read what they were writing.

Now Bob was an interesting character. His family was on welfare and only his older brother had the gumption to get up and get a real job, got through school to become something. But Bob, to his credit, managed to make a living on the internet. Came up with an electronic gismo that he was selling on eBay.

But when the same problems we all were experiences happened, NAFT, he's forced, at the age of 26, to get his very first job with me. What I learned from him was he only made me $50.00 a week. He could only produce enough product to make his wage and only $50.00 more. He hated to go on house calls with me. And once, one of my customers called and said, "That guy is just like all the younger people I have had as employees, they just don't' want to work." She said that she hired people for a chain of clothing stores for young people and had to use younger people. But after just five hours of work they would be exhausted.

During his employment with me his car broke down and instead of repairing it, just gave it up. Now taking the bus to work from downtown LA, he could no longer work Saturdays, because there were less busses running.

Then, when he saw another employee was going to leave, the one that went on house calls with me, he up a quit too. Also notable about him was he could not work more than 4 or 5 days without something happening and missing work.

Mark was the brother of a very good employee who now works for the power company. He got a great job like his dad working for the city. But when Mark sent his brother in he said, "You don't have to pay him much." I was soon to find out why. I sent him to pass out promo material door to door. After being gone for many hours, I found out what he had done.

Instead of walking down the block in an efficient way, to pass out promo door to door, he instead walked the much longer route of going across the street from house to house taking twice as much time. But then, when he got hungry, he walked all the way from near my shop to nearly a mile away to have lunch at Bob's Big Boy restaurant. Did he bother to pass out promo on the way? Of course not.

And then there was Anthony who scrapped the side of the service truck, not once but three times, not bothering to mention this to anyone.

Chapter 10

The New Old Generation

I didn't realize that older people were changing too. I wasn't having a lot of luck training younger people so I took a chance on an older person, Randy. I began to notice that he would occasionally go into a rage over some minor thing. Like one day, he could not find the proper tool and he just went off yelling loudly, "I thought this was a professional place, why don't we have the right tools?" Of course I would buy the right tools and they would end up lost. So that was a continuing battle.

But one day we were on the road to a house call and my assistant always had the job of navigating. This was before GPS. I would always instruct people, when using the Thomas map guide, that when you get near the neighborhood, to stop looking at the map and notice the street numbers on the houses. Because if you were on a street parallel to the street you wanted, you could easily tell how far off you were. This customer had to leave and so we were on a dead line. He was off by a mile or more and knowing not to get him upset, I said calmly, "Remember when you get near the neighborhood to look at the house numbers to get your bearings." With that, he exploded into one of his rages saying, "Don't talk to me like a baby."

I said, I was just giving you some instruction. He then said, "Shut up." Don't say anything more. I asked how I was supposed to give instruction then? and he said, "don't say anything more." I dropped the subject.

This had to be handled though and I wrote this up and gave him a letter to be signed so that it was documented that he had been warned.

The next day I asked for the signed letter and he said he would have to run it by his legal person first and left to do so. We never saw him again.

Later doing some research, I realized that he lived on a steady diet of energy drinks and the side effects of those drinks is, they could trigger unpredictable rants and rages.

Mike also had a temper problem. He thought that the shop should stand by him no matter what. So there we were with a customer who had written a book on Yoga. You think she might have been cool and easy going? But no. After delivering her TV she wanted some other work done that we didn't have the training to do. It involved reprogramming a remote that could operated any equipment. You need special training to program such a remote. They had words and she wanted to throw him out of the house. I finally told him to just go to the truck. After calming her down and explain calmly that we were not trained to do that kind of work, I got paid and left. But Mike was nowhere to be found, he took a bus home.

The next day, he came back and all was fine, I thought, till one of our neighbors near the shop called and asked if our employees would not park in front of their home as they had three cars. I simply asked Mike if he wouldn't mind moving his car up 20 feet. He blew up, saying I was not standing by him, angrily left and we never saw him again.

You cannot have problems with your neighbors. They have in the past looked out for the shop when I'm not there. Especially, if they are also one of your customers.

Ken had been an engineer and older guy. But he could not remember to park the truck correctly in the parking lot. It would always be sticking out in the alley and the large delivery trucks had to keep coming in and asking us to move it back so they could make the turn.

He also had memory issues. He kept discharging capacitors with a wooden handle screw driver and getting shocked. Large voltages can travel right through a wooden handled screw driver. One would think that the first time you did that you would learn that lesson.

Ben was an older guy who already had a heart attack and no wonder, judging by what he eat. But he would show up late, then go out back and have a smoke. He could not make it more than 4 or 5 days either without missing a day. One day, his brother-in-law called saying he would not be in, he had gotten so drunk he puked all over his apartment. But even after having an angioplasty done he continued to eat crap, smoke and drink. But was trying to have another one done. He was even considering getting a free electric wheel chair so he could sell it on eBay and make a few extra bucks.

He was working there at the same time as Bob, (mentioned earlier) a younger person, who also was missing a lot of work. I started marking on the calendar a red ex when ever either missed work. Soon the calendar was turning bright red. And it was amazing how many days they both were out the same day, but they were not friends.

And one of the more recent employee incidents evolved two of my helpers. I had gone with one of them to help me pick up a heavy TV set. Then, I delivered it back with a different guy. While there, I sent him to the truck to bring in a part I needed to hook up her VCR when the customer said to me while he was gone, "It's good of you to hire people like that. I worked my whole life in the mental health field." Then she said, "And the other one too." Meaning, the first helper that came with me. I said, "This one has made a lot of money on the internet." She dismissed that, he had just gotten lucky. In fact he was posting some items for me on eBay and was making mistakes.

So, keep in mind, most of the employees mentioned here were only there for a short time as you could see that a problem was going to rear its ugly head. That ugly head often showed up in just a week or two and others in just 30 days.

You might ask, why didn't you just pay more money for better help? I could have probably found a better quality of employee if I could have paid more money for them. But as it became harder to make money, we had to cut corners.

And I had to do more of the work. So hiring more experienced staff was not in the budget. It would have certainly led to less stress but I couldn't see how it would have made us more money. So that was not an option, economically, that I could see.

Chapter 11

The Great Employees

Now we had some excellent employees as well. George, also a member of my organization and well trained on this new tech we were using, was an excellent bookkeeper and counter person. You would open up a file drawer and instead of all the files just crammed in there, the way I did it, they were all neatly arranged.

But he really shined one day when two rough looking guys showed up looking for trouble. Their mother was an accountant for one of our customers and she noticed two identical charges on her client's bill. So these goons were going to straighten it all out. They seemed to be high on something and George just calmly pulled the receipts and got them to see that our customer had two identical machines that had the same problem, so naturally the price was the same. He patiently got through to them and by the time they left we were all shaking hands and happy as a bug in a rug.

And when George left my employment he had written up his entire hat. So the next employee could just go down the list and take over the post without any problems.

Early on we used to send our toughest jobs to a guy that worked out of his home. Eli would just kind of laugh at us because he would already know what was wrong with a unit by the symptom itself.

He kept a file on any new problem that would show up and just go to his index card and it was fixed just like that. And no matter what, every repair was just $50.00. When he got out of the business, many years later, he moved to Las Vegas and became an oil painter.

Jerry, was a great bench tech on VCRs. But his financial situation was so bad that I would have to pay him every day because he was always behind in paying his bills. I had learned that back logs prevented new work from coming in.

It's a metaphysical thing that you just have to observe to see that it's true. So Jerry would put aside all the hard jobs, and because of the back log, new work stopped showing up. So he would pull an all-nighter and the next day have all the hard jobs finished. Then, work would flow in again. He didn't believe me when I told about this until the third time that it happened. Then he finally agreed that it was true.

Jim Bowles was also quiet a tech and a big wave surfer when he was younger. He did our camcorders and many other things as well. He had learned technicianing from a home study course.

Lloyd was with me to the end and worked there as a contracted tech for 17 years. Totally honest, as you can always tell with bench techs, because if everything is a major problem you know that just can't be. Everything is not going to be a major repair. He would always do any callbacks first, which is a great thing to do, because those are going to be your most upset customers.

So the sooner you handle those jobs the better for everyone. But unlike the degraded employees, that I mentioned earlier, Lloyd was just the opposite.

He had the ability to <u>intend</u> work. Whenever he was going to go on vacation, he would finish all the current work and his jobs would just stop coming in. You would look around the shop and all the carts, with TVs on them, would be empty. Then a few days before he was going to come back, it would flow in again. It's a metaphysical thing that you just have to observe to see that it's true.

And Raul was loved by everyone. He was a model employee, always on time. But what he did is what every business owner wants.

He learned his first post, got it down, then took on another post, then got that down. Soon he was handling many posts, handling the counter, ordering parts, giving estimates. That is how to become a valuable employee. And he was so good talking with people that, even the hard working people who take parts orders, were complementing our store, because he treated them like human beings and was never rude to them. He worked for me for at least 10 years.

Thomas Magoon, my son-in-law, was also excellent with customers and was my shop manager for many years.

Excellent on computers and tape duplication. He also worked there for more than a dozen years. He is now back in the termite business. I highly recommend his work in that field as well.

And lastly Eric Ahlroth worked for me off and on over the 35 years and was my book keeper and confidante. Always came up with the right solution when dealing with a dicey family, friend, customer or employee situation.

So we did have some great employees as well and I thank them all.

Four Arguments for the Elimination of Television
                                Czappa

Chapter 12

Customers

Now I do have to mention our customers in this because without them we wouldn't have been there very long. We mostly had great people who stood behind us, some since the old shop that I bought out 35 or more years ago.

One early customer called after buying her first VCR and asked why she couldn't get it to work. I said, "Ok, so you have it plugged in the wall?" Yes, "You have wire from it to the TV set?" No answer, then she says, "Oh, they have to be connected? Yes." Problem solved.

We got a service call from one customer who said, "I swatted a fly on the picture tube of my TV set and now the fly is inside the picture tube. So, when my tech came back from the service call he explained what had happened. When the customer swatted the fly, the juice from the fly had made a fly shaped image in the dirt that was on the TV's screen. My tech simply cleaned all the dirt off the screen.

One of my first employees reported doing a house call to an older lady. She came to the door in a negligee and while he was working on her set, he said, it just slithered to the floor.

Our early answer machine only recorded for a minute or two. So we get a message that fills up the tape, then he calls back, and he keeps talking and it goes to the end of the tape. This goes on for several more minutes, but after all that, he never leaves his phone number and he never calls back.

There were many people who tried to repair things themselves. One customer tried to put up his own TV antenna up, but he was trying to hold it up with string, instead of guy wire.

Many people tried putting up their own antennas and they didn't work. Often I would find some simple thing wrong, like it was facing the wrong direction, or parts of the antenna where not actually connected.

We had a guy who took his camcorder apart trying to repair it himself while under the influence, according to him, of LSD. That one did not make it.

There was the guy who tried to solder in a part to his radio with liquid solder. Liquid solder is a plastic product and does not conduct electricity.

One day a lady comes by asking if we had a large magnet. I said, "What do you need it for?" She said she was sewing and she felt the needle went into her stomach and thought she could get it out with a magnet.

Another lady asked to buy or rent a microwave radiation detector. I asked her what she needed it for and was told, she lived in a home for elderly people and the neighbor that lived above her told her, he was sending microwaves through the floor to harm her.

Then there was the house call I went on to repair a TV that was dead. On the floor I found cable lines and multiple extension cords all over the place. Tracing out the plug from the TV, I discovered that one extension cord, was plugged into itself instead of the wall socket. Well this just gave me an idea for an art piece, "A New Form of Power."

A New Form of Power　　　　　　*Czappa*

I went to a customer's home, rang the bell and heard, "I'll be right there." I waited and waited, rang the bell again, no answer, so I left. Later I called the lady and asked what happen? I said, "Someone said, I'll be right there." She said, "Oh, that was my parrot, he learned to say that from me."

On several house calls the following happened. You go to a home to repair a console TV. You kneel down to get behind it when you feel your knee get wet. Looking around you suddenly realize that they have never broken in the dog. He is allowed to urinate on the TV set, the furniture, anywhere he wants.

You would also be surprised to find out how many people are hoarders. Most homes or apartments I went into, were not like the people on that TV show about this subject where you are walking on a foot or two of trash, but there is instead, at least a trail running through the home to the TV set. But, no way to get behind it, or even get it out of the house.

Then there was the customer that brought in his VCR with roaches crawling out of it. Opening it up it was jam packed with them. We immediately put it in a trash bag and one of my employees took it home. He bought it from the customer, as I wasn't going to work on it. He filled the bag with Black Flag and let it sit for a month. Then he patiently cleaned them all out and ended up with a really good machine.

Another time I arrive at a house that wanted to rent a TV from us. They said the roaches got their other one. I get to the door and notice the old set sitting on the front lawn. A gorgeous young lady comes to the door and as I look inside their apartment, there is trash everywhere and I can see roaches crawling around, even during the day. It was such a weird sight to see, this beautiful girl surrounded by filth. Needles to say, I didn't rent them the TV set.

And then there was the lady whose apartment was filled with hundreds of stuffed animals, but there was at least an inch of dust on all of them. They hadn't been moved or dusted in years. You always returned to the shop with dust all over you.

And of course, I should be the one to talk, it is a constant battle to keep things moving because we take things in for re-sale and recycling, keeping up with all that stuff is really a challenge.

Chapter 13

The Beginning of a New Era

So as you can see it was getting harder and harder to run a small business. Our yearly graph was a rocket ride till around 1994. Then it starts going down year after year for the next 25 years. And the year before I sold it, in desperation, I put a newsletter out and a story in the local newspaper, the Tolucan, (also on Itex), that we might have to close.

And that brought in a ton of work. People that were putting off repairing something, brought them in before we closed. I also did an art auction of the art work. We sold 16 pieces at that art sale. Who would have thought saying you might have to close would work so well? And many of our regular customers stopped by and begged us not to close. Who were they going to go to?

And so we held on till the end of that year when the new owner showed up. Even though I had been advertising it for sale for years, there were only a few other people who even showed any interest. But the new owner had run a TV shop before and was a good bench tech, so I knew he could make a go of it.

So that is the story of ARC TV. I sold it and the new owner has some new ideas to keep it going. There is always a need and market for older quality products like vintage stereos, phonographs and antique tube radios.

There is always new things coming down the pike to. It's in his hands now.

This is also the story of thousands of small businesses all across the country who have experienced similar conditions. NAFTA and the other trade agreements didn't just do in manufacturing but hurt the service industry and the sales industry too. We used to make a $50.00 profit on a VCR. And in the end they were selling for $50.00. How many do you now have to sell to make up for that? Wards and Circuit City and many other large companies also failed for the same reason. And now even Walmart is being done in by Amazon. And notice how they are looking for more ways to put people out of work. Like, self driving cars and packages being delivered by drones. I wrote an economic formula that exposed the idea that the economy could grow by laying off people and lowering wages. (*It's included in the appendix*).

As consumers what did we get? Was it an asset to be able to buy a cheap product that doesn't last? I think the manufactures would like nothing better if we all have to buy everything all over again every few years. And think of what that does to the environment?

The business climate is always going to be changing and I guess if I had to sum it up, you just have to be on your toes and stick your beak in the water of the times you live in. Look for and take the opportunities when they arise. Being ridged is never a good idea. Don't think the government or anyone else is going to take care of you. Bless any assets and people that come your way and watch out for your potential enemies.

You might wonder how we got it all done and had such a good reputation with all this, but somehow we just muddled through. And the good employees, as usual, kept the ship from sinking.

So, I'm off to try some new things. First, I wrote this book and am looking into giving lectures on my Tech book, "Tech Techniques."

Also, I'm trying to find some new ways of selling all the art work that is now in storage and at my studio. Those pieces are still available and can be seen on my web site. I am open to reasonable offers.

Hope you enjoyed the book and have learned a few tips about running a business. And, there are some interesting things in the appendix too.

Please Stand By   *Czappa*

Chapter 14

What Could Have Been?

It could have gone another way. We could have had well made products that held up and were easy to repair. I wonder if anyone calculated, if you had the choice of paying a little extra for a product that would last or be able to be repaired economically, would people do it? I would have loved to just pay a yearly charge for software if they would just not change it so much and make me have to learn a new program all over again.

It might be a new economic system that didn't waste valuable resources. Instead we are paying for the product being made in huge factories, the fuel to deliver it to the USA, then transport it all over the country in trucks and rail cars. Then we have to go shopping for a new product and then throw away all the packing material. Not to mention having to learn all over again how to use the new product.

You know if you want to know how to make a good product, just look at the old stuff. See what door handles didn't break on a car, what belt held up, what lever didn't break. Study it and incorporate that in your product. We would commonly see things badly made. Like on a microwave door lever. The plastic was so thin that it would break in just a few year on some models. We would just glue it back on building it up and not only on the side that broke but on the other side too.

I never had one come back when I repaired I that way. Could have been made that way in the first place. Another friend of mine, Chuck, who is also a repair tech, was an engineer for many years. He would design a product, then accounting would come to him and say, ok what parts can you downsize. If you need a 1watt resistor but you can get away with putting in a ½ watt resistor, and you are building a 1000,000 units, that saving of .005 cents will add up. As well as the savings on all the other parts that got downsized. But some of those circuits will fail much sooner.
Well, someday, do to all the electronic waste, things might even change. They could be penalized for making crappy products.

And one last point, we now have a huge problem with plastic bottles. One of my first jobs was being a box boy. And at that time our soda bottles were simply returned to the super market, the truck that delivered the new product would take them back to the factory and they would be inspected and washed and re-used. Seemed like a pretty good system. It could have expanded to all bottles, pickles, tomato sauce, hot sauce and beer. You would think that it would be cheaper to clean a bottle rather then make a new one. Plus before being a box boy, I made extra cash taking back my neighbors bottles for them. But, that's another story.

That's all I got to say about that.

The end

The Media Feeding Frenzy   *Czappa*

Appendix I.

This is the letter we put on promo for new customers and printed in various publications

Why fix things?

I have been in the consumer electronic repair business since 1969. But only in the last few years have I noticed that I am being asked this one question now several times a day, "Should I fix it or buy a new one?" With the advent of cheap home electronics, VCRs, TV sets, stereos, and now even printers, fax machines and microwave ovens, people want to know what to do when their equipment breaks. To fix or not to fix, that is the question? Their dilemma is only compounded by the prevalence of cheap replacements on the market.

Well, at a time when we are being asked to separate our garbage for recycling, why are manufacturers urging us to just throw away that old TV monitor or VCR -- not recycle it but dump it in the nearest landfill? Just throw it away, even though it is full of toxic material, including lead, and other toxic stuff? Are the manufacturers actually urging us to just dump it, even though special precautions are now made (at huge expense) to get lead paint off of a house and have it carefully dumped in special toxic control sites? Not to mention there is now an added mandatory toxic fee charged on new TVs and monitors.

Besides the toxic issues, just consider for a moment all of the wasted energy and resources that go into making any of these products. Metals, plastics, IC chips, PC boards, all made using our resources and energy.

Not to mention the Styrofoam, cardboard, and fuel necessary to ship it, usually from Mexico or China. All to deliver you a poorly made product that now lasts only one or two years, and all too often, only six months. Then, you, as a consumer, are given the privilege to drive down to your local discount store and start all over again. Wasting more resources to acquire another product that may not last as long as the one you just tossed.

The quality of new products has been dropping for over 10 years now. Most products today only last 2 years or less before needing repair compared to ten years for products made a decade ago. When people discover this, they often mention the TV or VCR in the bedroom that lasted 15 years. This is because some of the best quality products were made in the 1980s. In the 1990s, as Wall Street thinking started driving the economy, quality went out the window. Welcome to the New World economy, driven by "the bottom line" to deliver you a poor quality item so some Wall Street stockholder can have a higher dividend on his investment.

About 30% of all TVs and stereos just need to have their circuit boards properly soldered. The reason they come un-soldered is the manufacturers are now making the circuit boards by putting parts on both sides of the circuit board so that they will not have to drill as many holes. Because of this, they can no longer dip the circuit board in solder as they used to do or they will destroy the parts they put on the bottom. Instead, they are sprinkling the board with a poor quality solder dust and melting it with a type of blow dryer device. The connections come un-soldered in just 2 years instead of lasting 10 or more years like they used to do.

This is all done in order to bring you that cheap TV, although this same poor way of soldering is done on the more expensive models, too, so they don't last much longer than the cheap ones.

This problem is readily repairable by soldering the broken connections by hand with the proper solder; the way circuit boards should be soldered. When done properly, your product can easily last 3 times longer than when it first left the factory.

The second most common defect is, the manufacturers often put in a few undersized or low quality key parts, which promptly fail. Once these flawed parts are replaced with a quality part, your machine can last longer the second time around, sometimes by many years. We are actually in the business of re-manufacturing electronic equipment when you get down to it.

And consider this, another 30% of all broken VCRs, CD players, DVDs, fax machines and printers are not broken at all but just need <u>a good cleaning</u> and nothing more.

What is the solution to all this? Don't give up on your equipment so quickly. Have it checked by a competent repairperson first. Spare our environment from more toxic waste. And, as most electronic manufacturers are now foreign-owned; taking your money out of the country, investing in a repair is good for our "local" economy. Save yourself some money, too. It is often the cheaper option because our American ingenuity can make it better and last longer, saving you money and energy in the long run.
The end

<u>Appendix ii</u>

This is an example of the pink card that we inserted into the news letter.

**VCR or DVD
Heads / laser
Cleaning special
$27.50
This card is good for one Professional head
Cleaning on any VHS VCR brought to our
Store. Also good for DVD, Camcorders &
CD laser cleaning. This is an $11.00 savings
Off our regular price. Head and laser
Cleaning is always free with any
major or minor repair.**

2529 W. Magnolia Burbank, Ca. 91505

*This card is
   Good forever.
Or the end of time!*
        (818) 848-9998

Appendix iii

This was our flyer for new customers. The other side would have our letter, 'Why Fix things.'

More Junk Mail

Yes, it's more junk mail but what the heck, how are we going to let our neighbors know we are here and ready to service their TVs, VCRs and Camcorders or sell them new or rebuilt equipment if we don't say something?

Anyway, if you don't already have a reliable TV or VCR service man, give us a try. We are the TV store of choice of NBC Studios and have been servicing Disney, Warner brothers and many other businesses and over 12,000 of your neighbors since 1965. In fact we have repaired over 40,000 units since 1983 alone.

We have fully qualified expert technicians who are factory trained. So we can provide expert service faster and for less money than most factory service centers charge. And in spite of what Circuit City salesmen say it is almost always cheaper to repair than replace. Our techs can repair Camcorders and Big screen TVs the right way. And by the way, properly cleaned mirrors and lenses on a Big screen TV can add over 30 percent to its brightness and clarity, have you ever had yours cleaned?

If you are in the market for a new TV, VCR or Camcorder, come and see us first as not only do we have very competitive prices; we can clue you in to which companies are selling dogs. And a dog TV or VCR will bark all the way to the repair shop.

And if you are tired of paying high cable rates consider having us repair or install a new antenna for you. TV reception is free and most areas can get all of the lower broadcast channels 2 thru 13 plus many UHF channels for a tenth of the cost of those ever increasing cable rates.

So let us know if we can be of service to you. Your inquiries are always welcome. Please look over the complete list of services and sales items below to see if there is anything you need or want and visit our web site for more data. If you don't need anything now save the pink discount card for later.

SERVICES:

Televisions   All makes and models serviced. We make home service calls or you carry in and save even more. We also repair remote controls.

Big screen TVs   We have expert service on Projection TVs, all makes. We clean mirrors and lenses.

VCR'S   All makes and models serviced, including 3/4". Installation and operations explained.

Stereos   AM/FM, CD's, Cassette & speakers. Phonographs are our specialty.

Antennas   VHF, UHF, and FM antennas sold, serviced and installed. Cable line extensions and repair.

Camcorders   We have expert techs who can repair your camcorder fast and the right way.

Microwave Ovens   All makes and models serviced we do built-ins too. Apartment management accounts.

Computers & Monitors We repair computers, Laser and regular printers and monitors. Fax machines serviced too, all makes.

Film Transfers Transfer your 8-mm home movies to video. Audio and video tape duplicating. We also repair broken audio and videotapes.

SALES:
New Units TV, VCR and Camcorder sales (Zenith, Panasonic, Hitachi, Goldstar and many more).Competitively priced. We can probably beat anyone's prices on Big screen TVs and Camcorders. Industrial and broadcast quality TV's, VCR's, camcorders and editing Equipment.

Reconditioned   Quality reconditioned TV, VCRs, stereos, CD, cassettes and more. Fully guaranteed and at great prices. Ask us why our used equipment is better than new

Attachments   TV antennas and parts, VCR hook-up cables, VCR Plus, blank videotapes, tape re-winders, camcorder accessories, tripods & batteries

RENTALS:
A/V Rentals Overhead projectors, 35mm slide and 16mm audio projectors, TVs, VCRs and Big screens. TV, VCR   Microphones, amps, stereos and others. Camcorders Weekend, weekly, daily and monthly rentals.

   (818) 848-9998 * 2529 W. Magnolia Blvd. *
Burbank, California 91505
Home page: http://www.relaypoint.net/~arctv

Appendix iV

This is our thirty day thank you letter mailed to every customer that showed up. On the reverse side we would put a very short story to get them used to seeing them. It was called a thirty day letter because we would mail it within 30 days of them picking up their unit or order.

          "The Service, Rental and Sales People"
Dear Customer,
     We want to thank you for using our store recently, whether for a repair, rental, purchase or tape duplication. It was for a repair or sale item we hope all is well with it. If there is something wrong, please don't hesitate to let us know. We want everyone to be happy with our repair and sale items. Please don't wait until the warranty is up to get it checked out, especially camcorders. Remember most parts we install are guaranteed 90 days and labor on what we repair is 30 days.
     Also, a lot of people don't realize the extent of the services we offer. Besides repairing TVs, VCRs and other electronics, we also service microwave Ovens, stereos, phonographs, cassettes, CDs and much more. We also rent all kinds of equipment, from camcorders to microphones, amplifiers and speakers for sale and training seminars and Big screen TVs for those major sporting events! And we duplicate and repair both audio and videocassette tapes.
     So thanks again for your time and please look over the list below to see if there is anything else we can help you with.

If you don't see it just ask and please visit our home page too.

TVs & Plasma, LCD   All sizes, makes and models of TVs. Big screen and projection TVs. We do home service calls or bring it in and save. We offer pickup and delivery at a nominal charge too. We also install Plasma and LCD TV sets on walls.

VCRs & DVDs   All makes including 3/4" professional machines and time lapse. From head cleaning to a full rebuilding, our service is fast and efficient. One day DVD & VCR cleaning.

Stereo & Audio   All makes and models serviced. CDs, cassettes, tuners & amps. We also specialize in repairing record players and tube amps too. We fix speakers and answering machines.

Microwaves   We repair all makes and models of microwave ovens and do house calls on built-ins.

Computers & Printers   We repair Computers, printers, and laser printers and fax machines.

Antennas & HDTV   We repair and install antennas, repair and run cable lines, and hook up TVs, VCRs, stereos and surround sound systems. We are HDTV antenna experts.

Sales New and Used   We sell new and rebuilt TVs, VCRs, and stereo equipment. We are a Zenith, LG, Toshiba, Mitsubishi dealer and sell, Pioneer and many other makes. Check our prices on Plasma and LCD HDTV's. Our prices are competitive with the Big guys and our equipment is more often newer and fresher.

Audio & Video   We rent, slide, 16mm film and overhead projectors. Video projectors, Big screen TVs,
Rentals   DVDs, VCRs Camcorders, Plasma and LCD TVs.

Tape Duplication We make copies of tapes, even European and copies of your old 8mm or 16mm movies film to tape or DVD. They make great gifts. We also make audio copies to and from CD Phono and reel to reel.

Lamps & Small   We fix lamps of all sorts, toasters, hair dryers, curling irons, phones and many others

Appliances Odd items - just call and ask, we once repaired a bird incubator.

eBay Posting   We post items you want to sell on eBay for you from electronics to antiques. Our service includes photographing, packing & shipping. Call us for pricing and details. We purchase to.

Recycling   We are an approved electronic waste recycling drop off center. Safe recycling at no charge. TVs, printers, lamps, stereo, DVDs and most other electronic waste accepted.

Art   We are the oldest art gallery in Burbank showing the internationally sold California Assemblage Sculptures of Bill Czappa. Web site:
www.czappa.com
ARC TV & VCR, 2529 W. Magnolia, Burbank, CA 91505   Tele (818) 848-9998

Appendix v

This is one of the short stores we would put on back of our 30 day letter listing all the things we do.

Baseball

I don't know. Suddenly, it just hit me. I'm not sure if it was this summer and the Fourth of July that triggered it, or what. But there it was, just like that, right out of the blue, like a bolt of lightning! I was starting to *like* baseball.

Well, I don't mean that I would actually go to a game or anything, or listen to it on the radio or read about it in the newspapers, but just the same, I was beginning to just, well, *like* it.

I always liked that other people like it. It's just so American. I mean, I always felt better knowing that other people enjoyed it and what would summer be without it anyway? It would be a summer without flies, watermelon or cold beer. Not always in that order, however.

This all started on my first real job. I made gloves for my aunt and uncle for a dollar an hour. That's when a dollar was worth a dollar -- not a dollar twenty or fifty-two cents, but "exactly" one dollar. They had a little store right across from the Helms Bakery building on Venice Boulevard. It was called the "Banneck Glove Company." That was when Helms was still making donuts and bread. I guess they stopped making donuts 'cause they stopped making bread.

Well, I worked in the back room, just me and a six hundred degree boiler pressing gloves over a very hot metal hand, thinking of surfing and my girlfriend, but not always in that order. And in the other room was the thud sound of my Uncle cutting leather with a mallet and next to him was my aunt on her sewing machine, sewing up those pieces of leather into gloves.

But in between those sounds was the haunting sound of Vince Scully on the radio calling out the plays. And in between all that clamor was my aunt yelling back at the radio, cussing out Drysdale. She'd say, "Why the hell they leave him in so long? He's only good for five innings! Why the hell they leave him in?"

Well, someone else would get a hit off him and she'd be at it again. This time a little louder, "Damn it, why the hell they leave him in, he's no damn good." Then she'd light up another cigarette and uncle Casey's mallet would thud down one more time, and I'd press one more glove and summer would just creep on by like that, mallet by mallet, glove by glove, cigarette by cigarette, and play by play.

Well, I liked that. I mean, I really like that they liked baseball but I had other things to think about, like surfing and my girlfriend, but not always in that order.

And these days, I'll think about that girlfriend and surfing but I like baseball just a little bit more, not that I would actually go to a game or anything, or listen to it on the radio or read about it in the newspaper. I just sort of *like it* a little bit more.

The End   **William Czappa**

Appendix vi

This is an example of our full newsletter and a Christmas story

An RCA Hollywood Christmas !

I was thinking about the holidays this year and my thoughts wandered back to one of my very first jobs with a major corporation. In fact, come to think of it, that was the only job I had with a major corporation. It was the RCA Color TV service company in Hollywood California. This was probably the best and easiest job anyone could ever have, probably as easy as being president or the head of General Motors. One of those cushy jobs you never forget and will never ever find again. Now my cohorts in this story were Charlie Muir and Paul Scott. Charlie was not only a Fraternity brother but also a schoolmate going back to Daniel Webster Junior High. We both took Electricity 101 together with Mr. Payton and it was there that we learned (in just 3 painful weeks) how to strip the insulation off of a piece of wire real, real good. Paul and I went all the way back to Betsy Ross grade school in Culver City where we learned how to daydream and look at girls real, real good. It was Charlie who first got a job at RCA and then recommended Paul and me for a position as "Color" TV repair technicians. Now back then color was king. This was before computers and if you could fix a "Color" TV, you were the man. Of course when computers came around many TV techs learned how to fix them too just to amuse themselves.

There were so many aspects to this job at RCA that were great. Like, we had to drive a long distance to get there, which gave us the opportunity to ride our motorcycles to work each day. When you ride a bike to work, the further away it is, the better. Except or course, when it rained or was just too darn cold (as it often got as we approached the Holidays). Then we would take my 1953 Buick Special instead. It's funny, now come to think of it, the 53 Buick was a hand-me-down from my father which he drove to work too, down that very same street years earlier. He took Venice Blvd. to downtown and I would veer off to Hollywood. Yes, "Hollywood," tinsel town, tuff town, my town.

Now I remember the shop executives at RCA wanting us to pick up our service calls from the dispatcher and to get on the road as fast as possible each day. I remember rushing into work along with all the other techs and stopping by Rosie's desk.

Along with her regular duties (which I never could quiet figured out what they were), ran the coffee and donuts concession each day. Rosie would diligently collect our dimes and nickels, which would be used to pay for the annual Christmas party at some swank hotel. Well, to 19-year-old boys, that sounded like a deal. To have coffee and donuts and then get to go to an office party with all the cute secretaries? We would have been glad to pay a lot more for those darn donuts.

As I said, we all rushed in, got our calls, and then rushed out just as fast. Most of the techs just rushed right down the street to the coffee shop where they proceeded to have a real breakfast. That is, a real long, long breakfast (like 4 hours long).

You see, a good tech would get 8 service calls a day and you could usually knock them off in about 3 hours, unless they gave you a picture tube job to do, then it could take 3 ½ hours. They really didn't want you to come back for more calls, as there would not be enough for the next day. I tried to once. Sandy, the dispatcher, just said, "Why don't you go and have yourself a nice cup of coffee." That was the longest 3-hour cup of coffee I ever had.

This was a union shop, but unlike the well-paid unions, like the United Autoworkers Union, for instance, we got paid crap. But, hidden in our paltry benefits, we did get a light workload. In fact they could have fired half the techs and then there would have been just enough work for everyone left.

Well, I was not one for sitting around chewing the fat for hours each day, so I decided to use my time more wisely and, well, build a boat. As everyone else headed off for the coffee shop I rushed out to do all my service calls and then head back to Culver City, by noon, to work on my cruiser. Paul Scott's mom agreed to let me use her garage and driveway to build it, not realizing how large it was going to be. She was thinking "row boat" and I was thinking "Cabin Cruiser." My intention was to build this ship and live on it in the newly built Marina Del Ray boat harbor. I also intended on having lots of bikini clad babes on board as often as possible to. I didn't actually know how to get bikini-clad babes aboard yet, but I did know how to build an ocean going vessel. And I was sure that if I did that, the bikini-clad babes would soon follow.

Now in order to pull this off I was going to have to get my calls done really fast.

I had the Beverly Hills-Hollywood route and often some of those calls were way up on top of the hills overlooking Hollywood.

So, I got to be a pretty good driver and only got one ticket the whole time I worked there. But, one day the manager, "Sid Callen" called all us techs in for a shop meeting and proceeded to describe what he had seen a few days earlier. He said, "I walked out of the building a few days ago and I noticed one of our service trucks coming around the corner…on two wheels?

It then proceeded to almost run me down, then turned the other corner, … "on two wheels," and then entered the back lot coming to a screeching stop. As he described this event I realized that among these 30 or so techs present he was actually talking about me! I had delivered a TV set, but forgotten the remote, and in my hurry to get done (and most important back to the boat for some more "boat building") created the as-for mentioned incident.

It was almost as bad as the "special" meeting called because Charley Muir's truck had, let's say, become a trash dump! He often would have a late afternoon snack of KFC or Pioneer Chicken and would never bother to throw anything out. The truck just continued to fill up with chicken bones, skin, boxes and wrappers. Well, it was as high as the seat and reached all the way to the back of the van. I mean he really loved his chicken. I must admit it was a lot to handle in the hot summer months. But as we approached the chilly Holiday weather, which had a tendency to keep the decomposition process and gasses down to a minimum, it was really nothing to much to mention.

So, Charley could not understand what all the fuss was about. He saw nothing wrong with chicken bones and wrappers falling out of the door every time he got in or out. He of course also worked the swank, litter free, chicken bone deprived, homes of Beverly Hills.

Now, Paul was no angel either. He rushed out to the local coffee shop one morning leaving his tools back at the shop. He had to go back to the shop to retrieve them in order to make his first service call of the day at around 3:30!

We could never understand why the managers just didn't come up and talk to us personally. They always had to have a whole "shop meeting" to tell us. It never did make sense but that's what corporations do. Thinking back, it was probably the Chicken Delight dinners they would buy us to eat after each meeting that made them call so many meetings. Union rules maybe? I don't know. I never found out.

So that's how my days went. Fixing TVs really fast, building the boat, and then hurrying back to the shop to check in. I'm not sure how many extra miles I put on that service truck or how much gas was wasted driving back to Culver City, but it must have been substantial. Things got even better working there just after Thanksgiving when a new secretary was hired and I couldn't keep my eyes off of her. After that, no matter what direction I went, there was something beautiful to see, "my boat" or back to work to see the "secretary."

She was the kind of girl that the other techs would kid about. They would make comments about her, they'd say, "She's, look, but don't touch." I thought, though, that she was just a little shy like me and I like that a lot. She was a little on the short side and I liked that too.

She had the greenest eyes I had ever seen and the cutest pouty-est lips. Lips that said, "These could be yours, just figure me out." Each day as I turned in my receipts to the cashier I would smile at her from across the office, she would smile back, and I would try to figure her out. The only thing I figured out though was her name, it was Marlene.

But, I was painfully shy and she was painfully beautiful. I had visions of her being my date for the shop Christmas party that was coming up soon. Then one day, as I returned from the field, she was standing by the back door and I actually mustered the courage to ask her out, although my question sounded more like a plea or casual remark or flippant comment and well, she said no. If she had said yes, I would have probably passed out. I was actually kind of relieved.

As we got near the holidays I took my mind off that incident by noticing how nice the homes I was going into, now decorated, looked. I even got to work on Dean Martins TV set. He was not home that day but his son was, (the one that died in the air force a few years ago). He was playing a drum set that was set up in the foray of the house. The foray was so large I thought I could put my whole boat inside of it. In fact I thought that, "This would be a great place to build my boat." I could put my table saw over there where the drum set is and move the kid up to his room. Dino could come down once and awhile and sing Valero while I worked. But how do I get it out the front door? I still do this when I go into anyone's house I figure out how I would arrange things, let's see, the Bar over here and the bikini clad babes over there.

Well, we finally arrived at the long awaited "Christmas Party" and everyone looked fine all dressed up in suits and ties.

The only thing reminding me that these guys were actually TV techs, were all the bald heads and well, the great jokes. I don't know why that is but there is an alarming number of TV techs that are bald. In fact one night, at the annual obligatory union meeting, the glare off all those baldheads sitting in that auditorium was blinding (the jokes weren't all that bad either).

Now, even though I was only nineteen, and since we were in a private room, I thought I might be able to have a real drink. Un-fortunately, after being asked for my Id at the bar, I had to ask for a coke instead. When I turned to go to my seat, Marlene was standing behind me taking it all in. I watched from my seat as I saw her buy a "real" drink and then it suddenly sunk in, she was 3 years older than me. It was not to be then nor later, I had been seeking an older woman and didn't know it. Charley thought it showed some balls though and was quiet impressed that I had even attempted to ask her out.

Soon after the holidays our union, The United Electronics and Feather Workers of America, went on strike or more accurately (to illustrate how bad our union was) we went on strike against our union and RCA. So, I realized, I may never see Marlene again. After the strike most of us techs realized we could make a lot more money, let me rephrase that, "a hell of a lot more money," not being in the union and many of us never went back.

Then one day, years later, after marrying and having moved to the San Fernando Valley, I ran into Marlene.

There she was working in the office of a jewelry store sitting behind a typewriter as I always remembered her. And there I was holding my newborn daughter, but somehow I could not look at her, I knew it was her and I knew she saw me but I didn't look her way again. I thought a lot about that afterwards. I thought this could have been her child I was holding. And years later when I had divorced the woman who bore that child, I thought, maybe if it had been her instead that would not have happened. Maybe it would have been different. We were only three years apart. What's three years in all of eternity? Just maybe, I would be going home to her for the holidays this year, that nymph of a secretary with her green eyes and pouty smile. Who knows, maybe things would have been spelled and punctuated a little better around here two.

The end   **Bill Czappa**

2004   **ARC TV Gazette**   **Circulation 10,000**

++

Well once again we hope you enjoyed our newest True Hollywood story and if any of you are getting duplicates or just don't like to receive mail, just let us know and we will be happy to take you off of the mailing list. Just call, email, write or leave a message on our machine. We have now over 10,000 people on our mailing list.

The full version of this story is also on the internet site with a few photos from Paul Scott showing the back of the RCA Service lot in Hollywood circa 1969 and me building my boat in his mothers driveway.

If you would like to read more of our stories or purchase a booklet of 36 of them they are still on sale at the shop for only $5.95. And if you are in the neighborhood stop in and see the new work in our art gallery.

You know ARC TV is also the oldest art gallery in Burbank now going on 21 years old. It was in the San Fernando Valley art tour this year.

Also if you are online visit our Web site as it has been recently redone with many new items we service or sale and twice the number of art works on display as well.

We now have our own web master working for us and so we have also ventured out into web design. If you need a whole site created or just a few items changed John is the one who can do it. We have continued to upgrade our tape duplicating equipment and can now handle more duplications and in even more formats as well, from your old home 8mm film movies to a simple VHS copy to DVD.

Now on to some tips that may save you money on repairs of your electronics.

Monster cables, at a monster price to pay.

Many people are spending huge sums on Monster cables to hook up their equipment.

I have seen people pay more for their cables than the DVD they are hooking them up to. It is really not necessary to use expensive cables to hook your DVD or VCR to your TV or surround sound system. I defy anyone to show me the difference in picture quality.

Although the Monster brand is made very well most TV's, VCR's and DVDs "aren't." People are breaking the RCA plugs right off their units when they try to take off a Monster cable. In other words we have reached the point where the cable to hook it up is built better than the thing being hooked up! To prevent this do not just pull a Monster cable off. Instead gently twist it as you pull.

And while on the subject, as the manufactures continue to produce crap the RF fitting on your TV and VCR is no longer put on very well either. They used to be soldered on. But no more time for that, they have money to make. My god you know what solder costs? Well, actually hardly anything. Go figure. I was going to make a joke saying that if they make things any worse the buttons will be falling off then realized that we just had several Sharp Microwaves come in where the buttons did fall off. They were only six months old!

On camcorders.

Camcorders more than ever are very delicate devices and as such do not hold up well with sand in them or water either. So, when going somewhere dusty, windy or wet take the time to at least rap your unit in a clear plastic bag with rubber bands. You can do so in such a way as to not block the lens on most units and still operate the controls and see the viewfinder.

They also do not like extreme cold or heat. And why anyone would think smaller is better.

These new tiny little palm-camcorders are not made very well. They are extremely fragile. These are not well made items.

HDTV update As predicted by me the date for the changeover to HDTV has been postponed till 2010. So there is no hurry to rush out and buy HDTV. So the pressure is off.

Zenith and LG

Zenith now has offered a second line of TV's called LG. So don't be confused if you start hearing about this new line it is not new it is Zenith and we just signed up to be a new LG distributor.

All The Things We Do

TVs All sizes, makes and models of TVs. Big screen and projection TVs. We do home service calls or bring it in and save. We offer pickup and delivery at a nominal charge to.

VCRs & DVDs

Camcorders

All makes including 3/4" professional machines and time lapse. From head cleaning to a full rebuilding, our service is fast and efficient. We offer one-hour head cleaning on request. We service all makes of camcorders VHS, 8 MM, Digital 8, Mini DV and even digital still cameras.

Stereo & Audio	All makes and models serviced. CDs, cassettes, tuners and amps. We also specialize in repairing record players. We fix speakers and answering machines, too.
Microwaves	We repair all makes and models of microwave ovens, too, and do house calls on built-ins.
Printers & Monitors	We repair Computers, printers, laser printers, computer monitors and fax machines.
Computers	We now can build a whole web site for you are just change a few pages call for more info.
Antennas & HDTV	We repair and install antennas, repair and run inside cable lines, and hook up TVs, VCRs, stereos and surround sound systems. We are the HDTV antenna experts.
Sales New and Used	We sell new and rebuilt TVs, VCRs, and stereo equipment. We are a Zenith Dealer and sell Panasonic, Quasar, Toshiba, Pioneer and many other makes. Check our prices on Big screen TVs and HDTV. Our prices <u>are</u> competitive with the big guys and our equipment is more often is newer.

Audio & Video	We rent Video, Slide, 16mm film and overhead
Rentals	projectors. Big screen TVs, Camcorders,
Amps	mics, flip charts and more for weddings, parties and sales-training meetings.
Tape copies	We make copies of tapes (most formats, even European) and copies of your home movies. We also make audio CDs from cassette or reel to reel.
Duplicating	8mm or 16mm movie film, too. They make great gifts. We also make audio copies to Cassette or CD.
Lamps small	We fix lamps of all sorts, toasters, hair dryers and other odd things to
Appliances	just call and ask.

ARC TV & VCR, 2529 W. Magnolia, Burbank, CA 91505

Tel (818) 848-9998 - fax (818) 848-4036

E Mail arctv4@relaypoint.net   Home page: http:www.relaypoint.net/~arctv

Appendix vii

Other examples of short stories I wrote this one could be used anytime.

Finding Ginger

I think it important to mention that sometimes my stories are made up or embellished but I have to say this one is an entirely true story. It took place just after the holidays and I was at a friend's house for a party. I was showing off one of my new artworks there and we were having a few drinks. Well, all was going fine till this girl walks in the room and our eyes met, well more like locked. She was my ideal idea of a woman. Her tight, short, silky, lacy, frilly, black dress left nothing to the imagination. Her curves were all in the right places and exactly the right size. Her clothes seemed to be enjoying themselves. She looked like a mixture of Fergie from the Black Eyed Peas, Carmen Electra, Sherilyn Fenn from the movie, Boxing Helena, and several girls I had known in college. She was one of those girls a little on the short side, not bony, that had a little baby fat. She also had fantastic green eyes. I tried to make the perfect woman once with Photoshop. I scanned in those three women together but when I was done it looked like Betty White.

I asked a friend who she was and he said, "That's Ginger, she's getting divorced." Well as the evening progressed she seemed to be well attended but I couldn't help notice her furtive glances and eventually I ended up talking to her. She was fascinated with the artwork I had brought.

As we talked I could tell we would become an item. She said she loved how the work, not only gave off smoke and had moving parts, but she really loved my creative use of pasta.

Later I ended up in another room of the house and discovered my friend Brian was concerned that we had been spending too much time together. It was apparent he was very interested in her as well. I said, "Brian, aren't you happily married?" He said, "But just look at her." There was another guy following her to with that lustful look in his eye. I asked who he was and Brian said "Oh that's her brother."

As Ginger came back in the room I then became aware that every guy in the room was looking at her, even Tipper and he was gay. As the party continued Ginger and I kept trying to find a place to be alone. We walked casually from room to room chatting but every room we went through guys were hoping to have some time with her and their girlfriends or wives seemed to be annoyed.

We finally found a secluded place in the foyer and she said, "I am sorry about that" (meaning all the attention from the other guys), "I'm a bit of a flirt. But I think there is something very special about you." She said this while looking deep in my eyes and I just grabbed her and kissed her deep and long.

We then held each other and she started to lick my ear. I wanted to kiss her again but she just kept it up. Then suddenly I woke up, my dog Muffin was licking me trying to wake me up as I was late.

As I drove to my studio I couldn't help thinking how real this dream was. I couldn't get her out of my mind.

A week went by and then I got a call from a collector, he said he wanted to see my work and I set up an appointment for him to come in.

I said, "How about Thursday?" Thursday's always a good day for an appointment, it's not the beginning of the week and if it goes bad you have Friday and the weekend to get over it.

He arrived and with him was his wife, Ginger. She was the girl I had just dreamed about. He introduced me to her and I shook her hand, but she held my hand a little longer then was comfortable, since her husband was standing right there. I just couldn't break the stare that we mutually were embracing. I knew it was the girl I had dreamed about and wondered if she knew as well.

He said his wife had seen my work online and wanted to see it and show it to me in person. As I showed him the piece Ginger was most interested in (the one she liked in my dream) she was fondling him but flirting with me in the most obvious manner. She rubbed her hand up and down his arm standing real close and posing. She excitedly told him how the piece produced smoke, had moving parts and she loved the clever use of pasta.

Then she asked to use the ladies room. Jack then said "That was a show just for you, you know. Don't worry though, we're getting divorced. We will always be friends but we can't get along.

The final papers will be signed next week. Somehow she got really interested in you and your work about a week ago; she just can't stop talking about it."

When Ginger returned he told her he was buying the piece for her as a divorce gift. She was ecstatic. He then said, "I have another appointment. Why don't you get to know each other and show her the rest of your work and if you wouldn't mind could you drive her home? We live near here in Toluca Lake." I said I would be glad to and he left. I casually put up the closed sign and turned off the phone.

As I strolled with her around my studio showing her the rest of my work, she put her hand around my arm and stood very close, taking every possible chance to look deep in my eyes with a look that said, "I'm all yours." I finally couldn't take it any longer and just pulled her close to me and gave her a deep long kiss. We embraced and as we did I could smell her hair, but it smelled a little like doggy shampoo. This was confusing but somehow I didn't mind. She began to lick my eyelids. I thought "Well this is interesting," and as she continued to lick them, I woke up. Muffin, my dog, was trying to wake me, as I was late for work.

On the way to the studio I was still thinking of her and as I came to a stoplight. I looked in the Lexus next to me and there she was. She turned; saw me and I could tell she was surprised to see me too. We both knew that what happened, had happened. As the light turned she gave me a little wave and I waved back. Her husband was driving, they turned left and I never saw her again. His license plate read "Woof Woof."

But I could still hear her hot, sultry sexy voice in my head when she described my piece - "I love how it produces smoke, has moving parts, and that ever so clever use of pasta."

The End   **William Czappa**

Appendix iv

A Summer story

The Bar-B-Que

I don't know if it was now or later that I became aware of the "bar-b-que" but when it happened is not important, only that it did. So many years and so many steaks and chickens later, I still reflect on those morsels that went before. But in these years, I must say that those years seemed better and indeed they were, since everything is better when you are eight, and it's the Fourth of July.

A month earlier our parents had sent out invitations to all our friends and relatives to come to a "shindig" -- a shindig, they called it. But to me it was the Fourth of July and cousin Carl was going to be there, my ol' buddy, friend and life-long pal. The adventures we had and were to have put Hollywood to shame. But we didn't think or know so then. It was life that showed us the truth.

As the day approached and school ended, I realized that I would not see Peggy (the class sweetheart) again for several months. I thought that I had better turn my attention to something real and reachable, like the Fourth of July, rather than daydream about the impossible Peggy.

That was a good idea and one that I wish I kept, but unfortunately lost in later years.

Well, as the weeks passed and the day approached, the arrangements kept piling up in anticipation. I was in charge of the yard. I began watering the lawn daily so that on the final day it would be as green as our '53 Buick. I had planned to cut it the morning in question so that it would have the most profound effect on our guests.

The patio had needed painting and several weeks before my sister, father and myself had gotten all the paint we had on hand and painted each of the scribed imitation flagstone panels a different color: the colors that would reflect the fireworks we already saw in our dreams.

Time grew closer and then suddenly it was the morning of the Fourth and we had lots to do. The brick icebox, my father had built into our patio, had to be washed out and filled with ice, soda and beer and, of course, the lawn, now very green, had to be cut one last time. Our Doughboy pool had to be cleaned and the bugs removed from the surface, and the most fun of all was, the hamburgers had to be made.

This year, my father had made a hamburger press and I couldn't wait to use it. It was made out of wood and two coffee can lids that pressed together. I would lay out two pieces of wax paper with some hamburger in between and presto, it was like magic! Perfect burgers.

The day started like that and went slowly, much more slowly than now. The guests would not arrive till about noon and there was still the long wait till dusk and the fireworks.

Then Carl showed up and the day was complete. My ol' buddy, friend and life-long pal was there. The day could begin. We swam for hours and all the grown-ups joined us with movie cameras whizzing.

My father ran and dived in over the side of the pool. We still have film of that momentous event. Well, all the swimming just made us even more hungry and the burgers began to sizzle over the charcoal grill. The charcoal was not the same either. We didn't have these perfect little cubes like today. No, they were real pieces of charred wood, hard to start, but somehow it was better, more natural than today. Anything real is better as we should all have learned by now.

We ate and ate the corn on the cob, and the potato salad, which I still do not like but am glad that others do, as it seems a necessary and important part of barbeques that maybe someday I will appreciate and perhaps someday will even try again.

Well the party rolled on and me and cousin Carl ate our food sitting in my soup box racer as his father rolled lit cherry bombs under my car to our delight and fear, as we realized they were dangerous, our hands showing small signs of blood.

After more cider and more fun the night began to come, which was necessary to conclude the grand finale of this glorious day.

A day we would remember for all of our lives and would never be repeated again in quiet the same way, no matter how we tried.

And at last, at the very last moment, the most astounding thing happened. My friend, who lived across the street and a few doors up, (just cross the city line) was also enjoying the fourth with his family and relatives, who had bought even more and bigger and better fireworks than we had, came to talk to us. Fireworks were not legal in LA where they lived, so we all agreed that they should bring their party, (and especially their fireworks) to our house in Culver City where God lived and made the laws.

Days earlier my dad had made a special stand to shoot off the "cones," and "pinwheels" on, and as the sun set, in the last moments, the men began to hammer up the final touches to the upcoming display. We had already lit our "worms" and "Smoke Houses" and were beginning to set off our "Sparklers" as the sun finally set.

Then it began. The sun was gone and the first of three hundred and fifty two fireworks we now would share in turn did their thing, and I might add, for a longer period of time then today. And, yes, us kids did count every one of them, several times.

When we ran out of "Piccolo Petes," we would scream them out with our mouths and would be echoed by others blocks away doing the same thing.

But the "Pin Wheels" had not yet been torched, nor had the big "Cones" or the "Roman Candles," as the night went on seemingly forever.

So much smoke began to float down the street, from others doing what we were doing, it seemed like the city had been fogged in and the air was thick with gun powder and smoke.

Well, I don't remember how that night ended. Perhaps it never did or maybe I still want to savor all the fun we had. But it does live on in my memories and I know that someday it will happen again. So I keep watering the lawn and cleaning the barbeque, just in case. And I wish I could find some apple cider that tastes as good.

The End

Appendix ix

A Catalina Christmas

I was nearly 21 when the following incident happened. I was in my third year of a two-year college and living on a boat that I built in Marina Del Rey. Up to that point in my life I had never missed a Christmas with my family and later with my close friends. And so it would be a big deal for me to just ignore the holidays as my parents had instilled in me, as it was something they could not live without. Growing up and helping them over decorate the house and yard each year was something even I looked forward to, even when I was no longer a kid. And I kept up this holiday spirit going probably in an effort to somehow keep my dad's spirit alive after he passed away. So I have always had something to do or somewhere to go for Christmas. I even got a small Christmas tree for my boat.

That's my boat

But this year things had changed; I had just lost my girlfriend Candy Wayne. You know, losing a girl friend just before the holidays is just not the thing to do and looking around I realized my prospects for having close company, family and a holiday feast, something I always enjoyed, were getting pretty lean. And no one was planning to be at the fraternity house either on Christmas day.

Steve Rice invited me to go with him to Las Vegas and stay at his mother's place, but I just had that experience the previous year. We were to fly there, have a fine turkey dinner at a good restaurant and see the town. But unbeknownst to me, once Steve and his mom had a few drinks and started talking, no one was going to go anywhere. So we had Wild Turkey for dinner instead. And to make things worse, they didn't have any mixer.

They were straight drinkers. And so it was pretty sad the day after Christmas when we finally did make it to a restaurant and I ordered turkey. The waitress had this look of pity on her face' but I was a traditionalist and I had to have at least one bite of turkey on Christmas or at least soon after.

So this year, feeling rejected and forlorn, I decided that I would forgo my usual Christmas celebrating for once and see what it was like to spend it all alone for a change. And the most alone place I could think of was Catalina Island in the winter. So it was on that Christmas Eve afternoon,

I boarded my boat, a 22-foot cabin cruiser and headed for Catalina Island all by myself.

It was always dangerous to take a small boat out there even with a crew. I didn't have a marine radio or even flares and cell phones hadn't been invented yet. There was always just enough gas to get me there and back.

One slight mistake, just ten degrees off course and I would be found deep at sea eaten by penguins. I was even relishing that prospect, that'll really make Candy feel sorry I thought. I hadn't learned yet that the person doing the dumping never gives a thought about you again.

Well, I knew of a somewhat protected cove we had just visited last summer called "Goat Harbor." I would go there. I had aboard turkey helper, cranberry sauce and a can of black olives. I just couldn't give up on all of my holiday traditions you know, those family customs run deep.

Yes, I would go to that bay, throw anchor and have my holiday meal out there alone in the wilderness.

I left early enough to get there before the sun set. The trip up the coast was fine and going across the channel the water was pristine. But I had a ominous feeling, as it was a little too smooth, a little too glassy, especially for a cold winter afternoon. My boat was not a deep V hull made for ocean travel but really a lake boat with a planning hull and on a glassy day like this it got up and rode on top of the water. I got there in no time. But, just after anchoring things changed. The wind came up and the waves became larger. I had to set a second anchor.

I settled down for the night, although settling was not the right word, as the swell were getting bigger by the minute and I found myself in the middle of the night having to make a sea anchor from the canvas from my fish tank. It worked by keeping my bow into the incoming swells but soon after that my camper propane heater gave out and I realized it was going to be a very cold holiday. I put on my sailor cap and got out my best nautical jacket.

I thought back to my friends on shore and wondered what Candy was doing with her new boy friend. She was probably snuggled up against him in front of a warm fire. I found some solace in the fact that she didn't even know where I was or what I was doing.

And somehow that thought made me even more determined to stick it out. There is a small reward for wallowing in self-pity and remorse and the environment I was in was helping with that feeling quite a bit.

Well, I awoke the next day and it was still turbulent but a lot calmer than before. And as the morning wore on I began to realize that an adventure like this was really just not all that fun.

I put on an 8-track tape and the first song that came on was "Sloop John B." "I boarded the sloop John B, my grandfather and me."

And in fact, what was a wonderful bay in the summer time, was a hellhole in winter. It was a lonely and desolate spot to be in. Even the trees on shore looked lonely and forlorn. I thought about why Candy said she had to leave me. She had met another artist whose work spoke to her in ways that mine didn't. She said she just couldn't be with an artist who spent so much time making art out of pasta. She needed to be with a painter or at least a calligrapher. "Pasta," she said, "Would never hang in 'The Louvre,'" although it might be served in the cafeteria."

And so as I began to cook my Christmas dinner I turned on the radio and another song came on, Macarthur Park, "Someone left the cake out in the rain.... I don't think that I can take it, it took so long to bake it and I'll never have that recipe again...." That was it, that song always got to me, I just couldn't take it any longer. I had enough of this.

I pulled up all my anchors and headed for home. No matter what loneliness faced me back at the empty frat house it couldn't be any worse than this place and it would at least be warm. That is, soon as I got a bottle of rum and lit me a nice fire, urrr.

The waves in the channel were getting worse by the minute. Some were getting so large that when

I went over the crest my propeller would come out of the water. But I had a new determinism and I pushed that ocean going vessel through the waves on the straightest course I could manage,

I didn't want to spend one more minute at sea, I remembered my geometry, the shortest distance between two points was a straight line. And after two agonizing hours and short on fuel I was once again safe in the breakwaters of Marina Del Ray harbor and heading for my slip. There were penguins on the rocks eyeing me with a menacing look; they had missed out on a fine meal.

I immediately drove to the frat house to dry out, warm up and reminisce about my journey while nursing a beverage.

As I pulled up to the house I could see some people inside and one people was a very attractive young lady with long brown hair sitting in the window. She turned to look at me just as I got out of my 1953 Buick Special, our eyes locked and she gave me a big smile. I thought wow, this looks promising. Inside next to a roaring fire I found Jack Davies, one of my frat brothers. He was there with his girl friend Beverly and she had invited her friend Linda along. Jack immediately offered me an eggnog, heavy on the nogg. I was still dressed in my boating attire and sailor's hat and looked like something the cat dragged in. But Linda seemed to be spell bound as I told them my account of what I had just experienced.

Jack was a great storyteller himself but he also knew when to relinquish the floor. So as I talked Jack kept the eggnogs rolling.

Now Linda was just 18 and one of those girls that looked young for her age and even when she turned fifty she was still going to look young. She had green eyes and a smile that was infectious and flirtations all at the same time.

She was wearing a short but tight green silk dress that hugged her body like a politician hugging a campaign contribution. She was a vivacious flirt and had no qualms about sitting very close to me as I spun my tale. She seemed to be the kind of girl who appreciated an older mature man, I was after all going to be 21 in just 18 months and she seemed to be more than interested and maybe was even intrigued with my captain's persona as I was still wearing my captain's hat and pea coat. As I continued my story she moved even closer and I could feel her nylon clad leg rubbing up next to mine as I gazed into her perfect twinkling green eyes.

After telling them my tale, I asked Linda what she thought about an artist that might be going through a "pasta" stage in his career. She thought that was fantastic and mentioned she was half Italian and said she was considering changing her major to art. And with that I thought for a second about that cold forlorn bay I had just returned from and how fast my mood had changed. In just a few hours I had gone from the coldest bleakest place on earth to, well, Linda.

And after some more talk and some passionate handholding, I somehow knew that I would not be spending New Years Eve alone. A new song popped into to me head, "Linda Bells, Linda Bells, Linda all the way."

The End   **Captain William Czappa**

Appendix X

This is the treatment for a TV show I was encouraged to write by a working actor.

Willy's World

(Based on a true story)

W G A West
Registered 1483615

Willy's World is a TV comedy in serial form that follows the Walter Mitty type exploits of whimsical artist Willy Chappy, who owns a TV repair store in Burbank, California. Willy involves his young, often geeky, but hip employees in his surrealistic daydreams that come to life in separate sketches. The overly creative Willy imagines all kinds of scenarios from, how do you know you're not in a video game? To how to fix LA's broken rapid transit system, with the use of roller coasters running under those high voltage towers that run all over the city. In between these fantasy adventures, Willy deals with the humdrum, but often comical, world of a TV service center.

Some of the adventures are shot in reality show format and actually take place. In one fantasy adventure, Willy Suggests an art show by finding people to participate in it by drilling a hole in a phone book and then invite all people whose name got drilled through to bring in to a real art gallery whatever they consider their finest work of art. This episode is in the reality show format and an actual art exhibition is held, along with an opening reception.

Many episodes find Willy in his service truck training a new assistant to help him on service calls. He also uses the assistants to keep from being bored; he likes to bounce his newest hare-brained ideas off them. When he tells his assistant one of his numerous creative fantasy ideas, the scenarios then take place.

For example, he might say, "Can you imagine what it would be like if the government actually did a really good job? Take the DMV- it could be so much better than it is now; this is how it could be...

You show up and there's no line. A very nice looking woman, 'Beverly,' greets you and escorts you into her plush office. You are invited to sit back in a comfortable chair and on the desk is your favorite beverage, fixed just the way you like it.

Beverly asks about the kids and your job. She is very friendly and seems to know all about you. She quickly tells you that everything is ready; you just need to pass the eye test and have your photo taken. She points to a brooch that is hanging between her large breasts and asks, "Can you tell me what this says?" You read it aloud. It says, "You are a very attractive man."

Beverly then says, "Great, you passed the eye test. Now, for your photo. Look right here. Wait a minute," she says, "We can do better than this." She, presses a button on her desk and two more attractive women show up. One starts working on your hair, the other on your face. When they're done you look like Burt Reynolds. Beverly then says, "Now that's better, smile!" She sees that you're being a little shy, so she comes around the desk, and while nearly sitting in your lap, rubs her nylon clad leg against yours and says in a low, sexy voice, "Now I know you can do better than that, Joey."

Your expression changes, she snaps the photo and then says, "Got it." She presses a button and your new driver's license pops out. She says, "We'll see you in 4 years."

You go out front to get your car and it's brought to you by a valet. It has been washed and vacuumed. You get in and notice that it smells nice. You try to tip the attendant, but he refuses saying, "This one's on Uncle Sam Joey."

Back at the service truck Willy says, "Now that's how it could be." His assistant is thinking about this as they arrive at the service call they were heading to, he starts wondering, "Who is this guy?"

As the story unfolds you find out more about Willy. He opened the shop so that he could finance his art career, but he only has one day a week to make art. The store has become his gallery with art works on the walls and sitting on the TV sets that are for sale. The service business has become more complex than it used to be, and the shop is losing money. Many more situations come up with customers and employees.

He works at a tremendous pace and even though he is older the younger employees can't keep up with him. One time he asks an employee who is walking very slowly behind him, "What would happen if you walked faster?" And he's told, "I might fall over."

In between his work at the shop he buys supplies for his artworks. When UPS arrives it might be parts for a TV set or something unusual for one of his artworks. He has his new assistant call up a vendor he has found who makes fake eyeballs, and has him order some for a piece he is working on. The new employee says to another, confused, "I just ordered fake eyeballs?" He gets ideas for artworks, short stories, movies, ideas for YouTube, and even how to fix our economy while driving on service calls. Each one of these turns into a segment and is played out. What would happen if one of these guys asking for handouts on the street, instead of just asking for money, had a sign with a joke on it. One sign says, "What happened to the peanut when he walked down the street," he then flips the sign and it says, "He got Assaulted."

Would they make more handouts by giving some humor? So it gets filmed and we find out.

Locations and cast

The story line would include a few regular employees and involve new people coming in for several episodes. The main sets would be the service truck, TV shop, and his art studio, which is really ½ of his garage. The other half is full of his daughter's junk. His daughter, husband and four kids live there with him in a one-bathroom house, but he insists on calling the house his art studio. Some of the episodes involve Willy's four grandchildren, his daughter, and son-in-law. His daughter and her husband think he is wasting his time making art and don't understand it.

William Czappa, the series creator

Humbly submitted, I am merely an egg that has not yet hatched.

Appendix Xl

The Economic Formula.

As a small businessman it has been a necessity that I study the problem of our dwindling economy and I finally came up with the following data regarding this. I've found the basic factors that make a growing thriving "consumer" based economy. There are only three.

You need businesses located in that country that can produce goods and services that people need and want to buy and can afford.

You need people with <u>disposable</u> income to buy those goods and services.

And you need a currency that is stable.

These three factors alone make up the economic triangle. Most important, if you raise one leg of the triangle, the other two will rise. If you lower any corner of that triangle the others will fall.

You can then see for yourself whether any of the "solutions" the great economists, or politicians, come up with will actually work or just make things worse.

Let's take a look at a stable currency first. You cannot have a good economy in times of runaway inflation for instance, because business won't invest in countries that are in that situation as it's too risky. Or a business, already in that country, will not start a new line. So a government has to make sure the money is stable. They do that by not overprinting money for one thing. How they go about that further is another subject but it must be in control.

Now, by consumers, we are stressing people with "disposable" income. Not just people with enough money to get by and make ends meet, but people that are well paid. So, the more "disposable income" they have the more they can buy. The more goods and services they can buy the better the economy will be, as long as those goods and services are produced in that country.

This of course could be overdone and people can be overpaid, causing the price of a product to skyrocket or can even cause the business to go under and no longer be competitive, as has happened with our steel industry at one time.

Business's producing goods and services assumes that a company is making a product or service that people would need and want. It's also assumed they can make it in quantity without polluting the environment and killing off their consumers, or the cows. They would also need the people and resources to produce the product in abundance at a price that was viable. But most important is, that the factory is located in that country. You cannot have all your goods and services made in another country, or by robots, and think your country is going to be in good economic health.

So we see that for an economy to do well there must exist a balance between the company and its employees. If the company does not pay enough to their employees, they will not have enough money to buy other companies products or services. The companies, over all, will then have less money, as we have been seeing happen now for many years.

And that leads us to the heart of our current situation. Our corporations, through NAFTA (North America Free Trade Agreement) and other trade agreements, have been making sure the US consumer makes less and less money by shipping jobs out of the country and paying those left less and less money. This practice set in motion a dwindling spiral.

Some say that it was not fair for a 40,000 per year insurance salesman to have to pay more for a car because an autoworker makes $70,000 a year (Never mind that the price of cars has not dropped since most of the manufacturing of cars left the USA).

But, that $70,000 a year autoworker supported many businesses below him. Since he was a "consumer with disposable income" he was able to buy cars, houses, lawnmowers, garden furniture, put his kids in private school, and could afford to buy insurance. He also helped support the government by paying lots of taxes from income and sales tax. In other words, the money did trickle down under that scenario.

All one has to do is look at Flint Michigan to see that this is true. The auto industry there kept the whole town going. It wasn't just the autoworkers who lost their jobs when General Motors sent their jobs from Flint to Mexico. All the other businesses suffered too.

And why doesn't Mexico now have a thriving economy since they have all these great jobs? Well, they didn't pay the workers the same high rate of pay. They didn't create a "consumer with disposable income". How many new cars do you think an autoworker in Mexico will be buying at .80 cents and hour? I'm not sure even Coka Cola benefited. Would you pay an hour's work for a can of Coke?

Now the proponents of those trade agreements said that they were building markets in other countries. But the indicator of this is the Trade deficit, which continues to rise, showing that they did not accomplish that either. The trade deficit shows that we are now a nation that imports, not exports.

The only thing they successfully exported was lots of jobs and raw materials.

They also said that we were not going to be a manufacturing country anymore. We would be a sales and service country. Well, according to an article in the wall street journal, 50% of the companies that serviced things like, TV's, cameras, lawnmowers, washers and dryers etc, were forced out of business due to low prices of the items they were repairing.

Thus creating more consumers with less disposable income. Now, on the surface this seems great. There have been lower prices on "some" things, like TV's, VCR's, Camcorders, microwaves, washers, dryer's etc. But along with that decrease in price also came a decrease in quality and the longevity of the product too. Most products are now made to last only two years. So if you factor this in you will be repairing or replacing the item sooner. So, it is questionable if the consumer has gained anything in this area either.

According to this same Wall Street article, even if you want to repair something, it is getting harder to find someone left to repair it. And don't forget the cost to the environment, with all those now dumped TV's, VCRs and air conditioners filling up the dumpsites with toxic waste. And we have seen, recently, that they are being shipped and dumped to other countries, where they have now polluted their air and ground water.

The other problem is the cost has gotten so low in these areas that sales are also affected. A few years before Wards went under they were rated the highest seller of home electronics. How does the highest seller go under? They couldn't make a profit. We use to make a $50.00 profit on a DVD for example. Now the cheapest machine sells for $50.00. Now your profit is only what, $10.00 at best?

Now you have to sell 5 machines to make what you used to make on one.

So the number of units you sell may go up but your profit may actually be decreasing. And when people don't have good high paying jobs, there are not as many people able to buy as many of the higher priced units that they still make a good profit on.

Even the auto industry is crying that they no longer sell cars, they lease them. They would much rather sell them then lease them, as they have to carry the money for the loan.

Then, three years ago, we saw the next rung on the dwindling spiral take effect, many higher paid office managers lost their high paying jobs as companies lost more money. Of course they lost money; they laid off "consumers with disposable income."

Now these office managers will be buying less, causing the people and businesses they supported to do less trade, forcing another corner of the triangle to sag even lower.

Next on the ladder will be government jobs. Because the government pays its employees by collecting income tax and sales taxes, from working people in the private sector. We already see the government cutting back and making the fatal mistake of outsourcing some of these jobs to other countries.

Now it could have been true, what the proponents of these trade agreements were saying, if they had built markets in other countries and sold lots of goods and services, it would have raised one leg of the economic triangle here. Or would it have?

Since the factory was actually in another country

and the product was made by people in that country, the only benefit here would be those office workers and managers who they could not replace overseas or in Mexico. Most of the money would go to the stockholders and the company executives.

That would be an increase in income for some people. Put these are people who are already well off and don't go out and spend all of their income. They just buy more stock with it or houses in the Hamptons. How would that have trickled down to the autoworker in Flint Michigan though? It won't.

Now, how do you correct this? Well, businesses have to realize there is an economic triangle and therefore, their income depends on the ability of their customers to have "disposable income."

They have to realize that their own employees are indeed their customers as well. They have to stop being psychotic on this subject. They have to stop seeing employees as some nuisance that they need to get around somehow. Henry Ford knew that, why don't they get it?

When AT&T lays off 100,000 workers the executives at Ford probably think, "Their getting lean and trim, go buy some of their stock." When they should be thinking, "Holy Cow," their laying off our customers!

Uber and Amazons efforts to deliver people or packages by robots or drones, is going to hurt the economy, not make it any better. Elon Musk and the self driving truck is going to destroy the trucking industry. In fact there should be a penalty for any company that displaces a person with a robot. Maybe a high tax on them, since they will cause more people to be on welfare or living on the street.

Now if the intention of NAFTA was to really build up a market in some other country, and not just abuse those countries citizens, with just more low wages and long hours, then you have to pay them enough to be a "consumer with disposable income." As citizens we need to point this out to our elected officials, who in their mad scramble to get more campaign money from these same unthinking corporations, who do everything possible to lose us more jobs.

What we can do as shoppers is support local companies, buy American made products whenever possible and baring that, have things repaired by local service shops. Lacking this, the situation will continue to dwindle.

William Czappa

Post script

And what will the current huge tax cut do? Not much. The rich will just put it in the bank or in stocks, some corporations have already used it to buy back their own stock and the paltry sum everyone else gets won't be enough to do much good economically. But, because the debt will have to increase to pay for it all, we sit on the verge of the currency leg of the formula being destroyed.

And they are already talking about cutting programs for the poor and middle class. Which means, they will have less money to spend, as they try to pay for medical and other costs themselves. So that will not help the economy either.

A huge tax break for the poor and middle class would have of course done a lot more because that money would have been spent, thus aiding everyone's income, including the rich and the government. That money would have trickled up instead of down.

Other books by this author are available on Amazon.com

Tech Techniques
A book about his 50 years in the repair industry. Rules that you learn the hard way.

Holidaze
A book of his humor short stories about vacations and Holidaze while growing up in Culver City Ca. and being a single parent.

Assembled in America
A book about is career as and artist with autobiography and 50 photos of his work with explanations.

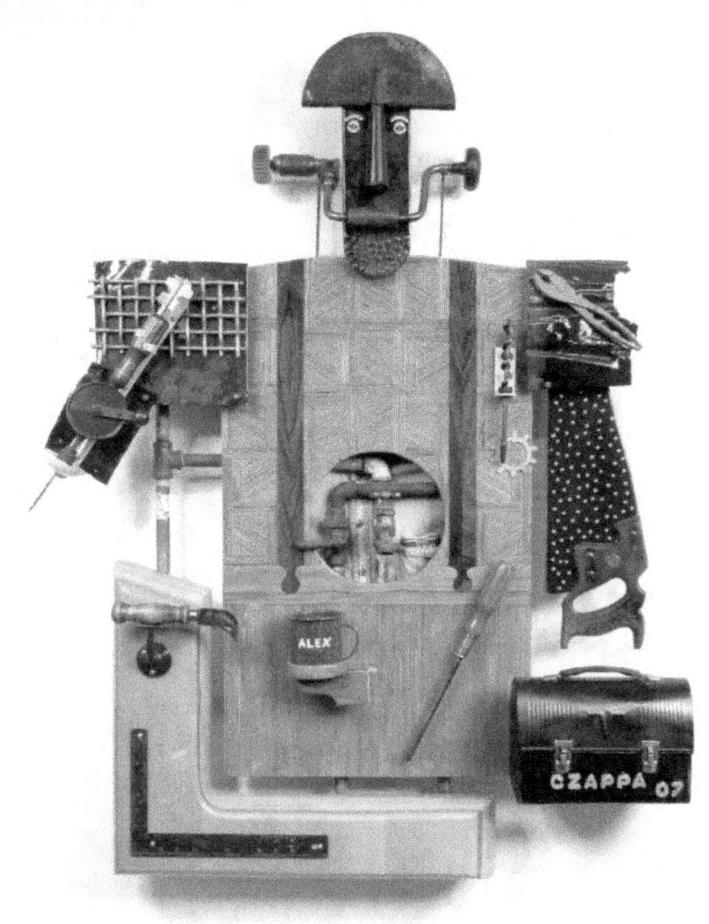

The Carpenter   *Czappa*

www.ingramcontent.com/pod-product-compliance
Lightning Source LLC
Chambersburg PA
CBHW071555220526
45469CB00003B/1026